Cosmic Pleasures

Sex Toy Astrology for Every Sign.

Matthew Petchinsky

Apophis Enterprises LLC

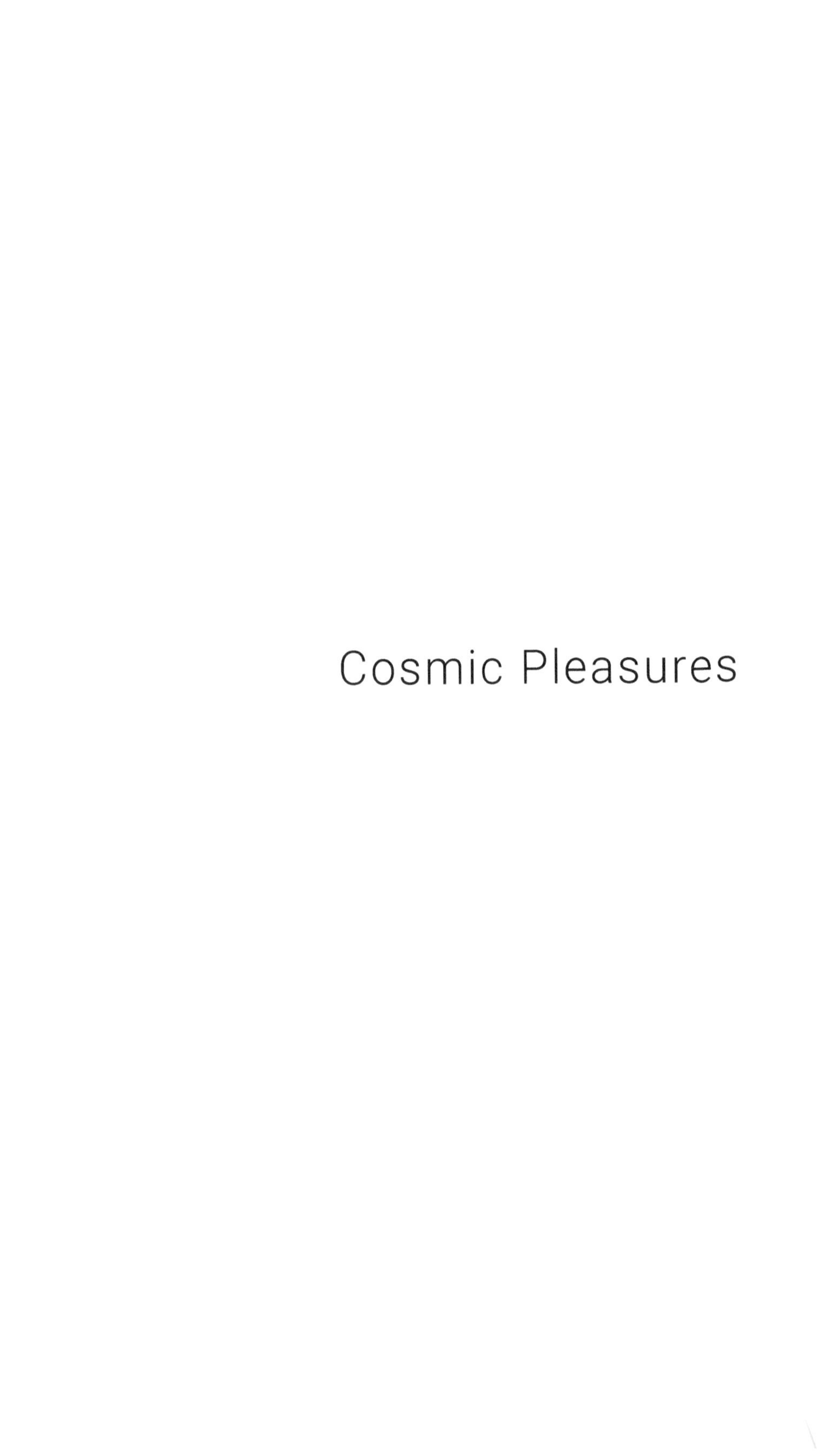

Cosmic Pleasures

Cosmic Pleasures: Sex Toy Astrology for Every Sign
By: Matthew Petchinsky

Introduction to "Cosmic Pleasures: Sex Toy Astrology for Every Sign"

Welcome and Explanation of the Book's Concept

Welcome to "Cosmic Pleasures: Sex Toy Astrology for Every Sign," a unique guide designed to enhance your intimate experiences through the powerful lens of astrology. Whether you're a seasoned astrologer or a curious novice, this book aims to connect the ancient wisdom of the stars with the modern world of sexual exploration. By understanding how celestial bodies and cosmic events influence your desires and preferences, you can unlock a deeper, more fulfilling level of intimacy.

In this book, you will discover tailored recommendations for sex toys and techniques based on your zodiac sign, moon phases, planetary alignments, and other cosmic phenomena. We'll delve into how each sign's characteristics align with specific sexual preferences and how you can use this knowledge to enhance your pleasure. Prepare to embark on an astrological journey that will not only enlighten you about your sexual self but also help you understand and appreciate your partner's desires.

Brief Overview of Astrology, Cosmic Events, Moon Phases, Planet Alignments, and the Wiccan Wheel of the Year

Astrology

Astrology is an ancient practice that examines the movements and positions of celestial bodies to understand human behavior and predict future events. At its core, astrology divides the sky into twelve segments, each associated with a zodiac sign. These signs—Aries, Taurus, Gemini, Cancer, Leo, Virgo, Libra, Scorpio, Sagittarius, Capricorn, Aquarius, and Pisces—are believed to influence our personalities, emotions, and behaviors.

Each zodiac sign is ruled by a planet that imbues it with specific traits. For example, Mars governs Aries, infusing it with passion and energy, while Venus rules Taurus, emphasizing sensuality and pleasure. By understanding the characteristics of your zodiac sign and its ruling planet, you can gain insights into your sexual preferences and how to enhance your intimate experiences.

Cosmic Events

Cosmic events, such as eclipses, solar flares, and meteor showers, have been revered throughout history for their powerful influences. These events can bring about significant changes in our lives, affecting our emotions, behaviors, and even our sexual desires. In this book, we will explore how these cosmic events can create unique opportunities for sexual exploration and growth.

For instance, a solar eclipse, which occurs when the moon passes between the Earth and the sun, can symbolize a moment of transformation and renewal. This can be an ideal time to try new experiences or rekindle the spark in your relationship. Similarly, meteor showers, known for their fleeting beauty, can inspire spontaneous and adventurous intimate encounters.

Moon Phases

The moon, with its waxing and waning phases, has a profound effect on our emotions and behaviors. Each phase of the moon—new moon, waxing crescent, first quarter, waxing gibbous, full moon, waning gibbous, last quarter, and waning crescent—carries its own energy and influences our sexual desires in different ways.

During the full moon, for example, emotions and desires are heightened, making it a perfect time for passionate and intense experiences. On the other hand, the new moon represents a time of new beginnings and introspection, ideal for exploring new fantasies or deepening your connection with your partner. By aligning your sexual activities with the moon phases, you can harness the lunar energy to enhance your pleasure and intimacy.

Planetary Alignments

Planetary alignments occur when planets position themselves in specific patterns relative to each other and the Earth. These alignments can create powerful energetic influences that affect our lives in various ways, including our sexual desires and experiences.

For example, when Venus, the planet of love and pleasure, aligns with Mars, the planet of passion and action, it can create an intense period of sexual attraction and desire. Understanding these alignments and their effects on your zodiac sign can help you make the most of these cosmic energies to enhance your intimate life.

The Wiccan Wheel of the Year

The Wiccan Wheel of the Year is a cycle of seasonal festivals that celebrate the changing seasons and the natural rhythms of the Earth. These festivals, such as Samhain, Yule, Imbolc, Ostara, Beltane, Litha, Lammas, and Mabon, are deeply rooted in ancient pagan traditions and are often associated with fertility, growth, and renewal.

Each festival on the Wheel of the Year carries its own unique energy, which can influence our sexual desires and experiences. For example, Beltane, celebrated on May 1st, is a festival of fertility and passion, making it an ideal time for exploring new sexual adventures and deepening your connection with your partner. By incorporating the energy of these festivals into your intimate life, you can create a more harmonious and fulfilling sexual experience.

How These Elements Can Influence Sexual Preferences and Experiences

The interplay between astrology, cosmic events, moon phases, planetary alignments, and the Wiccan Wheel of the Year creates a dynamic and ever-changing landscape that influences our sexual preferences and experiences. By understanding these cosmic influences, you can tailor your intimate activities to align with the natural rhythms of the universe, enhancing your pleasure and deepening your connection with your partner.

For example, if you're a passionate Aries, you might be drawn to sex toys that match your fiery nature, such as those designed for intense stimulation and adventure. During a full moon, you might find that your desires are heightened, making it the perfect time to explore new fantasies or try a new toy. When Venus aligns with Mars, you can harness the powerful energy of love and passion to create a truly unforgettable intimate experience.

By integrating the wisdom of astrology and the power of cosmic events into your sexual exploration, you can unlock new levels of pleasure and intimacy. Whether you're looking to deepen your connection with your partner or discover new aspects of your sexual self, "Cosmic Pleasures: Sex Toy Astrology for Every Sign" will guide you on a journey of celestial exploration and sensual delight. Embrace the cosmic energy and let the stars illuminate your path to greater sexual fulfillment.

Chapter 1: The Foundations of Astrology and Sexuality
Introduction to Astrology and Its Historical Connection to Sexuality

Astrology has been intertwined with human history for thousands of years, serving as a guide for everything from agricultural practices to personal relationships. Among its many applications, one of the most intriguing is its connection to human sexuality. Ancient civilizations, such as the Greeks, Romans, and Egyptians, observed the stars and planets to understand not only the cosmos but also the intimate aspects of human life. Astrology offers insights into our deepest desires, sexual preferences, and compatibility with others.

How to Read Your Astrological Chart

To delve into the world of astrological sexuality, it's crucial to understand how to read an astrological chart. This chart, also known as a natal or birth chart, maps the positions of the planets at the time of your birth and reveals your astrological makeup. Here's a step-by-step guide:

1. **Obtain Your Birth Chart**: You need your date, time, and place of birth to generate your chart. Numerous online tools and astrologers can provide this service.
2. **Understand the Components**:
   - **Planets**: Each planet represents different aspects of your personality and life.
   - **Houses**: The 12 houses represent different areas of life.
   - **Aspects**: The angles between planets, which affect how they interact with each other.

The Planets and Their Sexual Significance

1. **Sun**: Represents your core identity. In sexuality, it indicates your sexual vitality and overall approach to sex.
2. **Moon**: Governs emotions and subconscious desires. It influences your emotional needs and intimate connections.
3. **Mercury**: Affects communication and thought processes. It plays a role in how you express your sexual desires.
4. **Venus**: The planet of love and beauty. It's directly linked to your romantic attractions and sexual pleasures.
5. **Mars**: Represents drive and passion. Mars indicates your sexual energy and how you pursue sexual satisfaction.
6. **Jupiter**: Associated with growth and expansion. It influences your attitudes towards sexual exploration and boundaries.
7. **Saturn**: Governs structure and discipline. It shows your sexual boundaries and potential inhibitions.
8. **Uranus**: Represents innovation and rebellion. It affects your sexual uniqueness and potential for unconventional desires.
9. **Neptune**: Associated with dreams and illusions. It influences your fantasies and idealistic views of sex.
10. **Pluto**: Governs transformation and power. It's linked to your deepest sexual desires and transformative experiences.

The 12 Houses and Their Detailed Sexual Interpretations

1. **First House (Ascendant):**
   - **Overview**: Represents self-identity and physical appearance.
   - **Sexual Significance**: Indicates how you present yourself sexually and your initial sexual impressions.
2. **Second House:**
   - **Overview**: Governs values and possessions.

- **Sexual Significance**: Influences your sexual values and what you find sensually gratifying.

3. **Third House**:
    - **Overview**: Rules communication and thought.
    - **Sexual Significance**: Affects sexual communication and the sharing of fantasies.

4. **Fourth House**:
    - **Overview**: Represents home and family.
    - **Sexual Significance**: Indicates how your upbringing affects your sexual attitudes and needs for security in intimacy.

5. **Fifth House**:
    - **Overview**: Governs creativity and pleasure.
    - **Sexual Significance**: Directly linked to romantic affairs and sexual enjoyment.

6. **Sixth House**:
    - **Overview**: Rules health and daily routines.
    - **Sexual Significance**: Affects your sexual habits and how you integrate sex into your daily life.

7. **Seventh House**:
    - **Overview**: Governs partnerships and marriage.
    - **Sexual Significance**: Indicates your sexual approach in committed relationships.

8. **Eighth House**:
    - **Overview**: Represents transformation and shared resources.
    - **Sexual Significance**: Linked to deep sexual bonds and transformative sexual experiences.

9. **Ninth House**:
    - **Overview**: Governs philosophy and higher learning.
    - **Sexual Significance**: Influences your sexual philosophies and the pursuit of sexual enlightenment.

10. **Tenth House**:
    - **Overview**: Rules career and public image.

- ○ **Sexual Significance**: Shows how your sexual identity influences your public persona.
11. **Eleventh House**:
    - ○ **Overview**: Represents friendships and social groups.
    - ○ **Sexual Significance**: Affects how you view sexual relationships within social contexts and friendships.
12. **Twelfth House**:
    - ○ **Overview**: Governs the subconscious and hidden aspects.
    - ○ **Sexual Significance**: Indicates hidden sexual desires and potential for secret affairs.

Integrating It All: Interpreting Your Sexual Astrology

Understanding the planets and houses in your natal chart provides a comprehensive view of your sexual identity. Here's how to integrate this information:

1. **Identify Key Planets**: Focus on Venus, Mars, and the Moon for primary sexual insights.
2. **Analyze House Placements**: See which houses these planets occupy for contextual understanding.
3. **Consider Aspects**: Look at how these planets interact with each other (e.g., conjunctions, squares) to understand the dynamics of your sexual nature.

4. Aspects

Aspects are the angles formed between planets in your chart, influencing how they interact with each other. Key aspects to consider include:

- **Conjunction**: Planets are in the same sign, blending their energies. A conjunction involving Venus or Mars can intensify sexual desires.

- **Opposition:** Planets are 180 degrees apart, creating tension and balance. Oppositions can highlight areas of sexual conflict or attraction.
- **Square:** Planets are 90 degrees apart, indicating challenges and growth. Squares can point to sexual obstacles that lead to growth.
- **Trine:** Planets are 120 degrees apart, facilitating harmony and ease. Trines often indicate natural sexual compatibility.
- **Sextile:** Planets are 60 degrees apart, suggesting opportunities and support. Sextiles can enhance sexual creativity and experimentation.

5. Putting It All Together

Reading your astrological chart can initially seem complex, but breaking it down step by step will help you unlock profound insights into your personality and sexual inclinations. Here's a detailed guide on how to piece together the various elements of your chart to form a comprehensive understanding of your cosmic sexual blueprint.

Step 1: Identify Your Sun, Moon, and Rising Signs

The sun, moon, and rising (ascendant) signs form the cornerstone of your astrological profile:

- **Sun Sign:** Represents your core identity and ego. It's the most widely recognized aspect of your astrological chart and is often what people refer to when they ask, "What's your sign?" Your sun sign reveals your basic personality, including how you express yourself sexually.
    - **Example:** If your sun is in Leo, you might be naturally charismatic, confident, and enjoy being the center of attention. Sexually, this can translate into a desire for playful, adventurous encounters where you feel adored and admired.
- **Moon Sign:** Governs your emotional world and inner self. The moon sign provides insight into your emotional needs, intimate desires, and how you nurture and seek comfort in relationships.

- ◦ **Example:** If your moon is in Cancer, you may have a deep need for emotional security and intimacy in your sexual relationships. You might prefer gentle, nurturing sexual experiences that foster a sense of safety and connection.
- **Rising Sign:** Also known as the ascendant, this sign represents your outward behavior and how others perceive you. It sets the stage for your entire chart, influencing your approach to life and initial impressions in romantic encounters.
    - ◦ **Example:** If your rising sign is Scorpio, you might come across as mysterious and intense, drawing potential partners in with your magnetic allure and deep, probing nature.

Step 2: Examine the Positions of Venus and Mars

Venus and Mars are the key planets associated with love and sexual energy:

- **Venus:** Governs love, beauty, and pleasure. Venus's position in your chart reveals your approach to romance, aesthetics, and what you find attractive and pleasurable in a partner.
    - ◦ **Example:** If Venus is in Scorpio, you might experience love and attraction intensely, seeking deep emotional and physical connections. Your sexual desires may be transformative and passionate, with a focus on intimacy and loyalty.
- **Mars:** Represents passion, drive, and sexual energy. Mars's placement shows how you assert yourself, pursue desires, and express your sexual instincts.
    - ◦ **Example:** If Mars is in Aries, you might be bold, spontaneous, and assertive in your sexual pursuits, preferring direct and adventurous encounters.

Step 3: Consider the Houses of Venus and Mars

The houses that Venus and Mars occupy in your chart provide context for how their energies manifest in specific areas of your life:

- **5th House:** Associated with romance, pleasure, and creativity. Planets here can reveal your approach to dating and casual sexual encounters.
  - **Example:** If Venus is in the 5th house, you might be playful, romantic, and enjoy spontaneous sexual adventures. Your love life may be characterized by creativity and a zest for fun.
- **7th House:** Governs partnerships and long-term relationships. This house's influence highlights your approach to committed relationships and sexual partnerships.
  - **Example:** If Mars is in the 7th house, you may be driven to seek dynamic, passionate relationships and might find fulfillment in partnerships that challenge and excite you.
- **8th House:** The house of sex, death, and transformation. Planets in this house can indicate your deepest sexual desires and transformative experiences.
  - **Example:** If Venus is in the 8th house, your sexual experiences might be intense and transformative, seeking deep emotional bonds and exploring the darker, more mysterious aspects of intimacy.

Step 4: Analyze Significant Aspects

Aspects are the angles formed between planets, influencing how their energies interact. Key aspects to consider include:

- **Conjunction:** Planets in the same sign, blending their energies. A conjunction involving Venus or Mars can intensify sexual desires.
  - **Example:** If Venus conjuncts Mars, you may experience a powerful synergy between love and desire, creating a passionate and dynamic sexual expression.
- **Opposition:** Planets 180 degrees apart, creating tension and balance. Oppositions can highlight areas of sexual conflict or attraction.

- ◦ **Example:** If Venus opposes Pluto, you might experience intense, transformative sexual relationships marked by power struggles and deep emotional bonds.
- **Square:** Planets 90 degrees apart, indicating challenges and growth. Squares can point to sexual obstacles that lead to growth.
  - ◦ **Example:** If Mars squares Saturn, you may face challenges in expressing your sexual energy, requiring patience and discipline to overcome sexual frustrations.
- **Trine:** Planets 120 degrees apart, facilitating harmony and ease. Trines often indicate natural sexual compatibility.
  - ◦ **Example:** If Venus trines Neptune, you might experience a harmonious blend of romance and fantasy, creating dreamy and idealized sexual experiences.
- **Sextile:** Planets 60 degrees apart, suggesting opportunities and support. Sextiles can enhance sexual creativity and experimentation.
  - ◦ **Example:** If Mars sextiles Uranus, you may have an innovative and experimental approach to sexuality, enjoying spontaneous and unconventional encounters.

Example Chart Interpretation

Let's illustrate this with a detailed example:

- **Sun in Leo (5th House):** You are charismatic and enjoy the spotlight, with a playful and adventurous approach to sex. You thrive in romantic encounters that allow you to express your creativity and passion.
- **Moon in Cancer (8th House):** Your emotional needs are deep and intense. You seek profound emotional connections in your sexual relationships and are drawn to transformative experiences.
- **Rising Sign in Scorpio:** You exude a magnetic and mysterious aura, attracting partners with your intense and probing nature.

- **Venus in Scorpio (8th House):** You experience love and attraction intensely, seeking deep, transformative sexual connections. Loyalty and emotional depth are essential to your intimate relationships.
- **Mars in Aries (11th House):** You pursue your desires boldly and assertively, enjoying spontaneous and adventurous sexual encounters. You may be drawn to unconventional and innovative sexual experiences.

With this chart, you would likely benefit from sex toys that cater to both your need for deep emotional connection and your adventurous spirit. Toys that offer intense stimulation, such as those designed for deep internal sensations or adventurous play, would align well with your Scorpio and Aries influences. The combination of Leo's playful nature and Scorpio's depth suggests a preference for passionate and engaging sexual experiences.

By understanding your astrological chart, you can gain a deeper appreciation of your sexual nature and how to align your intimate experiences with the cosmic energies influencing you. This foundational knowledge will guide you through the subsequent chapters, where we explore tailored sex toy recommendations and techniques for each zodiac sign, helping you unlock the full potential of your cosmic pleasures.

'

Chapter 2: Understanding Sex Toys
Overview of Different Types of Sex Toys

Sex toys come in a wide variety of shapes, sizes, and functions, designed to enhance pleasure and explore different aspects of sexuality. This section provides a comprehensive overview of the main types of sex toys available, helping you understand their features and uses.

1. Vibrators

Vibrators are among the most popular and versatile sex toys. They use vibration to stimulate various parts of the body, including the clitoris, vagina, anus, penis, and nipples. Vibrators come in many forms:

- **Bullet Vibrators:** Small, compact, and discreet, ideal for clitoral stimulation.
- **Wand Vibrators:** Powerful and often larger, suitable for external stimulation of the clitoris or other erogenous zones.
- **Rabbit Vibrators:** Dual-action vibrators with a shaft for vaginal penetration and a clitoral stimulator, often featuring rotating or thrusting functions.
- **G-Spot Vibrators:** Curved to target the G-spot inside the vagina, designed for intense internal stimulation.
- **Panty Vibrators:** Wearable and remote-controlled, perfect for discreet public play.

2. Dildos

Dildos are phallic-shaped toys designed for penetration. They can be used vaginally or anally and come in various materials, sizes, and textures:

- **Realistic Dildos:** Molded to resemble a real penis, often with veins and a pronounced head.
- **Non-Realistic Dildos:** Abstract or artistic shapes, often colorful and textured.

- **Double-Ended Dildos:** Designed for simultaneous use by two people or for double penetration.
- **Suction Cup Dildos:** Equipped with a base that can be attached to surfaces for hands-free play.

3. Anal Toys

Anal toys are specifically designed for anal stimulation and come in various forms to cater to different levels of experience:

- **Butt Plugs:** Tapered toys that stay in place once inserted, used for prolonged wear or preparation for anal sex.
- **Anal Beads:** Strings of graduated beads that provide unique sensations when inserted and removed.
- **Prostate Massagers:** Curved to target the prostate (or P-spot) for intense internal stimulation.
- **Anal Vibrators:** Vibrating toys designed for anal use, offering additional stimulation.

4. Cock Rings

Cock rings are worn around the base of the penis (and sometimes the testicles) to restrict blood flow, leading to harder and longer-lasting erections. They come in various materials and designs:

- **Basic Cock Rings:** Simple rings made of silicone, rubber, or metal.
- **Vibrating Cock Rings:** Equipped with a vibrating component to stimulate the wearer and their partner.
- **Adjustable Cock Rings:** Designed with snaps or ties for a customizable fit.

5. Masturbators

Masturbators are toys designed to enhance solo play for people with penises:

- **Sleeves:** Soft, stretchy tubes with textured interiors that provide realistic sensations.
- **Fleshlight:** A popular brand of masturbators with lifelike openings and textures.
- **Strokers:** Compact, handheld devices that mimic the sensations of oral, vaginal, or anal sex.

6. Bondage and BDSM Gear

Bondage and BDSM gear are used to explore power dynamics and sensations in a consensual context:

- **Restraints:** Cuffs, ropes, or harnesses used to immobilize a partner.
- **Blindfolds:** Used to enhance other senses by depriving sight.
- **Gags:** Placed in the mouth to restrict speech and enhance submissive experiences.
- **Whips and Floggers:** Used to deliver controlled impacts for pain and pleasure.
- **Nipple Clamps:** Applied to the nipples to provide a combination of pain and arousal.

7. Remote-Controlled and App-Enabled Toys

These toys can be controlled remotely via a wireless remote or smartphone app, allowing for interactive and long-distance play:

- **Remote-Controlled Vibrators:** Ideal for couples, allowing one partner to control the other's pleasure.
- **App-Enabled Toys:** Offer customizable vibration patterns and can be controlled from anywhere in the world.

How to Choose Sex Toys Based on Personal Preferences and Needs

Choosing the right sex toy involves considering personal preferences, needs, and comfort levels. Here are some key factors to help you make an informed decision:

1. Identify Your Desires and Preferences

Consider what types of sensations and experiences you enjoy or want to explore. Reflect on whether you prefer internal or external stimulation, gentle or intense sensations, and solo or partnered play. This self-awareness will guide you toward toys that align with your desires.

2. Consider Your Experience Level

Your experience with sex toys will influence your choices. Beginners might prefer simple, non-intimidating toys, while more experienced users may seek advanced or multifunctional toys.

- **Beginners:** Start with basic toys like bullet vibrators, small dildos, or simple cock rings.
- **Intermediate Users:** Explore more complex toys like rabbit vibrators, prostate massagers, or vibrating anal beads.
- **Advanced Users:** Experiment with multifunctional toys, advanced BDSM gear, or app-enabled devices.

3. Think About Material and Safety

Sex toys are made from various materials, each with its pros and cons. Prioritize body-safe materials to ensure your health and comfort:

- **Silicone:** Non-porous, hypoallergenic, and easy to clean. Silicone is soft and flexible, making it a popular choice.
- **Glass:** Hard, smooth, and non-porous. Glass toys can be used for temperature play and are easy to clean.
- **Metal:** Durable, non-porous, and ideal for temperature play. Metal toys offer a firm and weighty feel.
- **ABS Plastic:** Hard, smooth, and non-porous. Often used in bullet vibrators and remote controls.

- **Jelly/Rubber:** Porous and may contain harmful chemicals. If choosing these materials, ensure they are phthalate-free and use with a condom for safety.

4. Size and Shape

Sex toys come in various sizes and shapes, catering to different anatomical preferences and experiences. Consider what size and shape will be most comfortable and pleasurable for you:

- **Vibrators and Dildos:** Choose a size that feels comfortable and pleasurable. Beginners might prefer smaller, slender toys, while those seeking more intense stimulation may opt for larger, girthier options.
- **Anal Toys:** Start with smaller, tapered toys if you're new to anal play. Gradually work up to larger sizes as you become more comfortable.
- **Cock Rings:** Ensure a snug but not overly tight fit. Adjustable rings can offer a customizable fit.

5. Functionality and Features

Consider what features and functionalities will enhance your experience:

- **Vibration Patterns and Speeds:** Some toys offer multiple vibration patterns and speeds, allowing you to customize your pleasure.
- **Remote Control:** Ideal for couples or discreet public play.
- **Waterproof:** Allows for use in the shower or bath and makes cleaning easier.
- **Rechargeable:** More environmentally friendly and convenient than battery-operated toys.

6. Budget

Sex toys come in a wide range of prices. Determine your budget and find a toy that offers good value for money. Remember that higher-quality materials and advanced features often come with a higher price tag but can provide a better and safer experience.

7. Read Reviews and Do Research

Before making a purchase, read reviews and seek recommendations from trusted sources. This can provide insights into the toy's performance, quality, and user satisfaction.

Conclusion

Choosing the right sex toy is a personal and exploratory journey. By understanding the different types of toys available and considering your preferences, experience level, and specific needs, you can select toys that enhance your sexual pleasure and align with your astrological profile. This foundational knowledge will empower you to make informed decisions and enjoy a fulfilling and cosmic sexual experience. In the following chapters, we'll delve into specific recommendations for each zodiac sign, helping you find the perfect toys to match your astrological identity and desires.

Chapter 3: Aries - Bold and Adventurous
Sexual Characteristics of Aries

Aries, the first sign of the zodiac, is ruled by Mars, the planet of action, passion, and desire. As a fire sign, Aries individuals are known for their boldness, adventurous spirit, and unrelenting energy. These traits extend into their sexual lives, making them dynamic and passionate lovers who crave excitement and novelty.

Key Sexual Characteristics of Aries:

1. **Passionate and Energetic:** Aries are known for their high energy levels and enthusiasm, which translate into a vigorous and lively approach to sex. They bring intensity and fervor to their intimate encounters, making them thrilling and unforgettable partners.

2. **Adventurous and Spontaneous:** Aries thrive on adventure and spontaneity, always eager to try new things and explore uncharted territories. They are open to experimenting with different positions, locations, and even toys, making their sexual encounters anything but mundane.

3. **Confident and Assertive:** Confidence is a hallmark of Aries sexuality. They know what they want and aren't afraid to take the lead in the bedroom. Their assertiveness can be highly attractive, creating a dynamic and powerful sexual experience.

4. **Independent and Self-Sufficient:** While Aries are passionate lovers, they also value their independence. They appreciate partners who can match their energy and enthusiasm but also respect their need for autonomy.

5. **Competitive and Driven:** Aries love a challenge and enjoy the thrill of the chase. This competitive nature can make their sexual

encounters playful and stimulating, as they strive to please their partner and excel in their performance.

Recommended Sex Toys and Practices for Aries

Given their bold and adventurous nature, Aries individuals are best suited to sex toys and practices that match their dynamic energy and desire for excitement. Here are some top recommendations:

Sex Toys for Aries:

1. **Rabbit Vibrators:** These dual-action vibrators provide intense stimulation to both the clitoris and G-spot simultaneously. Aries will appreciate the powerful, multifaceted pleasure that rabbit vibrators offer, satisfying their craving for intense and comprehensive stimulation.
2. **Wand Vibrators:** Known for their strong and rumbly vibrations, wand vibrators can deliver deep, satisfying pleasure to Aries individuals. They are perfect for external stimulation and can be used all over the body, adding an element of adventurous exploration.
3. **Remote-Controlled Vibrators:** These toys allow for spontaneous play and can be controlled by a partner, adding an element of surprise and excitement. Aries will love the thrill of unexpected pleasure, whether at home or in public settings.
4. **Cock Rings:** For Aries men, cock rings can enhance erections and prolong sexual activity, allowing them to fully channel their passionate energy. Vibrating cock rings can also provide additional stimulation to their partner, making the experience mutually satisfying.
5. **Anal Toys:** Aries' adventurous spirit makes them open to exploring anal play. Butt plugs, anal beads, and prostate massagers can provide new and exhilarating sensations, enhancing their sexual repertoire.

6. **Bondage Gear:** For those Aries who enjoy a bit of kink, bondage gear such as cuffs, blindfolds, and ropes can add an element of control and surrender, intensifying their sexual encounters.

Sexual Practices for Aries:

1. **Role-Playing:** Aries enjoy stepping into different personas and scenarios, making role-playing a fun and engaging way to spice up their sex life. Whether it's a dominant-submissive dynamic or a playful fantasy, role-playing can satisfy their need for variety and excitement.
2. **Outdoor and Public Play:** The thrill of potential discovery can be a huge turn-on for Aries. Engaging in sexual activities outdoors or in semi-public places can add a risky and exhilarating edge to their experiences.
3. **Spontaneous Sex:** Aries thrive on spontaneity. Surprise your Aries partner with unexpected intimate moments, whether it's a quickie in an unconventional location or an impromptu seduction at home.
4. **Competitive Games:** Incorporate playful competition into your sex life with games that have sexual rewards. This can be anything from strip poker to challenges that involve foreplay and teasing, catering to Aries' competitive nature.
5. **Intense and Vigorous Sex:** Aries have a lot of energy to burn, so intense, vigorous sex that allows them to fully unleash their passion and physicality can be incredibly satisfying. Positions that involve deep thrusting and active participation, such as doggy style or standing sex, can be particularly enjoyable.

Aries and Cosmic Events: Maximizing Pleasure

Cosmic events, such as planetary alignments, moon phases, and solar or lunar eclipses, can have a significant impact on Aries' sexual energy and experiences. Here's how Aries can harness these celestial influences to maximize their pleasure:

Moon Phases:

1. **New Moon:** The new moon represents new beginnings and is an excellent time for Aries to explore new sexual adventures or try out new toys. Setting intentions for your sex life during this phase can lead to exciting and fulfilling experiences.
2. **Full Moon:** The full moon amplifies emotions and desires, making it a potent time for intense and passionate encounters. Aries can use this energy to deepen their sexual connection with their partner, indulging in their wildest fantasies.
3. **Waxing Moon:** As the moon grows, so does energy and anticipation. This is a great time for Aries to build up sexual tension and excitement through prolonged foreplay and teasing, leading up to an explosive climax around the full moon.
4. **Waning Moon:** As the moon decreases, energy might wane slightly, making it a good time for Aries to focus on more intimate and nurturing sexual activities. This phase is ideal for connecting on a deeper emotional level with your partner.

Planetary Alignments:

1. **Mars Transits:** Since Mars is the ruling planet of Aries, its transits can significantly boost Aries' sexual energy. When Mars is in a favorable position, Aries may feel more assertive, confident, and eager to pursue their desires.
2. **Venus Alignments:** Alignments involving Venus can enhance Aries' romantic and sensual inclinations. This is an ideal time for Aries to focus on pleasure, beauty, and love, indulging in luxurious and sensual experiences.
3. **Eclipses:** Solar and lunar eclipses can bring about sudden changes and revelations. Aries can use these powerful cosmic events to

break free from sexual ruts and embrace transformative experiences that push their boundaries.

Seasonal Influences:

1. **Spring (Aries Season):** Aries feel most energized and vibrant during their own season, which coincides with the beginning of spring. This is a time of renewal and fresh starts, perfect for exploring new sexual horizons and embracing their bold nature.
2. **Summer:** The warm, lively energy of summer can amplify Aries' adventurous spirit. Outdoor sex and spontaneous encounters are especially appealing during this time, allowing Aries to fully embrace their passion and vitality.
3. **Autumn:** As the energy shifts to a more introspective and grounding phase, Aries can focus on deepening their emotional connections and exploring more intimate, slower-paced sexual activities.
4. **Winter:** The colder months can be a time for Aries to experiment with indoor activities and cozy, sensual experiences. Bonding over warmth and comfort can lead to deeply satisfying and nurturing sexual encounters.

Conclusion

Aries, with their bold and adventurous spirit, are natural explorers in the realm of sexuality. By understanding their key sexual characteristics, selecting the right toys and practices, and harnessing the power of cosmic events, Aries can fully embrace their passionate nature and enjoy a fulfilling and dynamic sex life. The following chapters will continue to provide tailored advice for each zodiac sign, helping everyone discover the cosmic pleasures that align with their astrological profile.

Chapter 4: Taurus - Sensual and Indulgent
Sexual Characteristics of Taurus

Taurus, the second sign of the zodiac, is ruled by Venus, the planet of love, beauty, and pleasure. As an earth sign, Taurus individuals are known for their sensuality, loyalty, and appreciation for the finer things in life. These traits extend into their sexual lives, making them deeply sensual and indulgent lovers who crave intimacy and comfort.

Key Sexual Characteristics of Taurus:

1. **Sensual and Tactile:** Taurus individuals have a heightened appreciation for physical sensations. They are highly tactile and enjoy the feel of soft fabrics, warm skin, and gentle touches. This makes them exceptional lovers who prioritize physical connection and comfort.

2. **Patient and Thorough:** Taurus lovers are known for their patience and thoroughness. They take their time to ensure their partner is fully satisfied, savoring each moment and building up to intense pleasure.

3. **Loyal and Devoted:** Loyalty is a cornerstone of Taurus sexuality. They are deeply committed to their partners and strive to create a stable and nurturing environment in their relationships. This devotion translates into a strong desire to please and be pleased.

4. **Indulgent and Luxurious:** Taurus individuals have a penchant for luxury and indulgence. They enjoy incorporating elements of beauty and comfort into their sexual experiences, such as candle-lit settings, silky sheets, and aromatic massages.

5. **Grounded and Practical:** Despite their indulgent nature, Taurus individuals are grounded and practical. They value reliability and consistency in their relationships, preferring steady and predictable patterns over spontaneous adventures.

Recommended Sex Toys and Practices for Taurus

Given their sensual and indulgent nature, Taurus individuals are best suited to sex toys and practices that emphasize comfort, luxury, and deep physical connection. Here are some top recommendations:

Sex Toys for Taurus:

1. **Luxury Vibrators:** High-quality vibrators made from premium materials such as medical-grade silicone or polished metal can appeal to Taurus's love for luxury. Look for vibrators with multiple settings to customize the intensity and pattern of stimulation.

2. **Body Massagers:** Full-body massagers that deliver soothing vibrations can enhance Taurus's appreciation for tactile sensations. These can be used for sensual massages that relax and arouse, creating a deeply intimate experience.

3. **Glass Dildos:** Glass dildos offer a smooth and firm texture that can be heated or cooled for temperature play, adding an extra layer of sensory pleasure. Their artistic designs also appeal to Taurus's appreciation for beauty.

4. **Clitoral Suction Toys:** These toys provide gentle, rhythmic suction that mimics the sensation of oral sex. The luxurious and precise stimulation can be deeply satisfying for Taurus individuals who enjoy slow and thorough pleasure.

5. **Weighted Kegel Balls:** For Taurus women, weighted kegel balls can enhance pelvic floor strength and increase sexual pleasure. The sensation of the weights can be both arousing and beneficial for sexual health.

6. **Cuffs and Restraints:** Soft, comfortable restraints made from plush materials like velvet or faux fur can add an element of excitement while still maintaining Taurus's need for comfort and safety.

Sexual Practices for Taurus:

1. **Sensual Massages:** Taurus individuals love physical touch and relaxation. Start with a full-body massage using warm, aromatic oils to awaken their senses and create a deeply relaxing and arousing atmosphere.
2. **Slow and Gentle Lovemaking:** Taurus prefers a slow and steady approach to sex. Focus on prolonged foreplay, gentle touches, and deep, rhythmic thrusts to build up intense pleasure gradually.
3. **Sensory Play:** Incorporate sensory elements such as silk scarves, feather ticklers, and scented candles to enhance the tactile and olfactory experience. Blindfolds can also heighten their sense of touch and anticipation.
4. **Bath or Shower Sex:** Taurus enjoys indulgent and luxurious experiences. Share a warm bath or shower with your Taurus partner, using the water and soap to enhance your connection and create a soothing, intimate setting.
5. **Food Play:** Indulge in erotic experiences involving food, such as feeding each other strawberries, chocolate, or whipped cream. This can combine their love for indulgence and sensual pleasure.
6. **Comfort and Safety:** Ensure the environment is comfortable and secure. Taurus individuals appreciate a stable and nurturing setting, so clean sheets, soft pillows, and a warm room can enhance their sexual experience.

Taurus and Moon Phases: Enhancing Intimacy

Moon phases can significantly influence Taurus's sexual energy and intimacy levels. Understanding these phases can help Taurus individuals and their partners enhance their connection and pleasure.

Moon Phases:

1. **New Moon:** The new moon represents new beginnings and introspection. For Taurus, this phase is ideal for setting intentions and exploring new aspects of their sexuality in a safe and private environment. Use this time to discuss desires and fantasies with your partner, setting the stage for future intimate experiences.

2. **Waxing Crescent:** As the moon begins to grow, so does energy and anticipation. This is a good time for Taurus to gradually build up intimacy and excitement. Focus on extended foreplay and gentle exploration, laying the groundwork for deeper connection.

3. **First Quarter:** The first quarter moon is a time of action and decision-making. Taurus can use this phase to actively pursue their sexual desires and take the initiative in their intimate relationships. Plan a special date night or surprise your partner with a sensual massage or a new sex toy.

4. **Waxing Gibbous:** As the moon approaches fullness, sexual energy and emotions intensify. Taurus can use this phase to deepen their connection through passionate and indulgent lovemaking. Experiment with different sensory elements and luxurious settings to enhance pleasure.

5. **Full Moon:** The full moon amplifies emotions and desires, making it a potent time for intense and passionate encounters. Taurus can fully embrace their sensual nature, indulging in their wildest fantasies and exploring new levels of pleasure with their partner.

6. **Waning Gibbous:** As the moon begins to wane, energy levels start to decrease. This is a good time for Taurus to focus on nurturing and comforting activities. Engage in slow and tender lovemaking, emphasizing emotional connection and intimacy.

7. **Last Quarter:** The last quarter moon is a time for reflection and evaluation. Taurus can use this phase to reflect on their sexual experiences, discussing what worked well and what could be improved. This is also a good time to reinforce the emotional bond with their partner.

8. **Waning Crescent:** As the moon approaches the new phase, energy is low and introspection is high. Taurus can use this time for rest and rejuvenation, focusing on self-care and gentle, intimate activities that promote relaxation and connection.

Conclusion

Taurus individuals, with their sensual and indulgent nature, thrive on physical connection, comfort, and luxury. By understanding their key sexual characteristics, selecting the right toys and practices, and aligning their intimate experiences with the moon phases, Taurus can fully embrace their deeply sensual nature and enjoy a fulfilling and pleasurable sex life. The following chapters will continue to provide tailored advice for each zodiac sign, helping everyone discover the cosmic pleasures that align with their astrological profile.

Chapter 5: Gemini - Curious and Playful
Sexual Characteristics of Gemini

Gemini, the third sign of the zodiac, is ruled by Mercury, the planet of communication, intellect, and adaptability. As an air sign, Gemini individuals are known for their curiosity, playfulness, and versatility. These traits extend into their sexual lives, making them dynamic and imaginative lovers who thrive on variety and mental stimulation.

Key Sexual Characteristics of Gemini:

1. **Curious and Open-Minded:** Gemini individuals are naturally curious and eager to explore new ideas and experiences. This open-mindedness makes them adventurous in the bedroom, always willing to try new things and experiment with different sensations.

2. **Playful and Fun:** Gemini's playful nature translates into a light-hearted and fun approach to sex. They enjoy teasing, flirting, and engaging in playful banter with their partners, making their sexual encounters lively and enjoyable.

3. **Versatile and Adaptable:** Gemini's versatility allows them to easily adapt to different sexual scenarios and preferences. They are equally comfortable taking the lead or following their partner's cues, making them flexible and responsive lovers.

4. **Intellectually Stimulated:** Mental stimulation is crucial for Gemini. They are aroused by engaging conversations, witty

exchanges, and intellectual foreplay. A strong mental connection enhances their physical pleasure.

5. **Communicative and Expressive:** Gemini individuals are excellent communicators. They are open about their desires and enjoy discussing fantasies and preferences with their partners. This clear communication helps create a fulfilling and satisfying sexual experience.

Recommended Sex Toys and Practices for Gemini

Given their curious and playful nature, Gemini individuals are best suited to sex toys and practices that emphasize variety, mental stimulation, and interactive experiences. Here are some top recommendations:

Sex Toys for Gemini:

1. **Bullet Vibrators:** Compact and versatile, bullet vibrators are perfect for Gemini's spontaneous and playful nature. They can be used for clitoral stimulation, teasing, and foreplay, making them a fun and essential addition to any sex toy collection.

2. **Couples' Vibrators:** Designed to be worn during intercourse, couples' vibrators provide simultaneous stimulation for both partners. Gemini will appreciate the interactive and shared pleasure these toys offer, enhancing their connection with their partner.

3. **Remote-Controlled Toys:** Toys that can be controlled remotely via a wireless remote or smartphone app add an element of surprise and excitement. Gemini can enjoy the thrill of unexpected pleasure, whether at home or in public.

4. **Anal Plugs and Beads:** For Gemini individuals open to exploring anal play, anal plugs and beads offer a new dimension of pleasure. Their playful nature makes them eager to experiment with different sensations and experiences.

5. **Nipple Stimulators:** Gemini's sensitivity to touch can be heightened with nipple stimulators. These toys can provide gentle to

intense sensations, adding variety and excitement to their sexual repertoire.

6. **Interactive App-Enabled Toys:** Toys that connect to apps offer customizable vibration patterns and can be controlled from anywhere in the world. This appeals to Gemini's love for technology and innovative play.

Sexual Practices for Gemini:

1. **Role-Playing and Fantasy:** Gemini's imaginative nature makes role-playing an exciting and stimulating practice. Whether it's dressing up in costumes or acting out fantasies, role-playing allows Gemini to explore different personas and scenarios.

2. **Dirty Talk and Verbal Play:** Engaging in dirty talk and verbal play can heighten Gemini's arousal. Their love for communication and mental stimulation makes this an effective way to enhance their sexual experiences.

3. **Spontaneous Sex:** Gemini thrives on spontaneity. Surprise your Gemini partner with unexpected intimate moments, whether it's a quickie in an unusual location or an impromptu seduction at home.

4. **Mutual Masturbation:** Watching and being watched can be highly arousing for Gemini. Mutual masturbation allows them to explore their own pleasure while simultaneously connecting with their partner.

5. **Teasing and Edging:** Prolonging pleasure through teasing and edging can be incredibly satisfying for Gemini. Building up sexual tension and delaying orgasm can lead to more intense and explosive climaxes.

6. **Sexual Games:** Incorporate playful competition and games into your sex life. From strip poker to sex dice, these activities cater to Gemini's love for fun and variety.

Gemini and Planet Alignments: Experimenting with Pleasure
Planetary alignments can significantly influence Gemini's sexual energy and experiences. Understanding these alignments can help Gemini individuals and their partners experiment with pleasure and enhance their connection.

Planetary Alignments:

1. **Mercury Transits:** As Gemini's ruling planet, Mercury's transits have a strong impact on their sexual energy. When Mercury is in a favorable position, Gemini may feel more communicative, curious, and eager to explore new sexual experiences.
   - **Example:** During Mercury retrograde, Gemini might revisit past sexual experiences or fantasies, reflecting on what worked well and what could be improved. This period can be an opportunity for introspection and growth in their sexual relationships.

2. **Venus Alignments:** Alignments involving Venus can enhance Gemini's romantic and sensual inclinations. This is an ideal time for Gemini to focus on pleasure, beauty, and love, indulging in luxurious and sensual experiences.
   - **Example:** When Venus forms a trine with Mercury, Gemini can experience a harmonious blend of intellectual and physical attraction. This alignment can lead to deep, meaningful conversations that enhance their emotional and sexual connection.

3. **Mars Transits:** Mars influences passion and drive, and its transits can boost Gemini's sexual energy and desire. When Mars is in a favorable position, Gemini may feel more assertive and eager to pursue their sexual desires.
   - **Example:** During a Mars sextile with Mercury, Gemini can experience heightened sexual energy and mental clarity. This alignment can be an ideal time for exploring

new sexual activities and communicating desires with their partner.

4. **Jupiter Transits:** Jupiter's expansive energy can encourage Gemini to explore new horizons in their sexual life. Alignments involving Jupiter can bring a sense of adventure and optimism, making it a perfect time for trying new things.

    ◦ **Example:** When Jupiter forms a conjunction with Mercury, Gemini can feel an increased sense of curiosity and a desire for growth. This alignment can lead to the exploration of new sexual techniques, toys, or practices.

Conclusion

Gemini individuals, with their curious and playful nature, thrive on variety, mental stimulation, and interactive experiences. By understanding their key sexual characteristics, selecting the right toys and practices, and aligning their intimate experiences with planetary alignments, Gemini can fully embrace their dynamic and imaginative nature and enjoy a fulfilling and adventurous sex life. The following chapters will continue to provide tailored advice for each zodiac sign, helping everyone discover the cosmic pleasures that align with their astrological profile.

Chapter 6: Cancer - Emotional and Nurturing
Sexual Characteristics of Cancer

Cancer, the fourth sign of the zodiac, is ruled by the moon, which governs emotions, intuition, and the subconscious. As a water sign, Cancer individuals are known for their deep emotional sensitivity, nurturing nature, and strong desire for security and comfort. These traits extend into their sexual lives, making them passionate and caring lovers who prioritize emotional connection and intimacy.

Key Sexual Characteristics of Cancer:

1. **Emotional and Intuitive:** Cancer individuals are deeply attuned to their emotions and the emotions of their partners. This emotional sensitivity makes them highly empathetic lovers who seek to create a strong emotional bond and ensure their partner feels cherished and understood.

2. **Nurturing and Caring:** Cancers are natural caregivers who enjoy taking care of their partners. They derive pleasure from nurturing their partner's needs, both emotionally and physically, creating a safe and comforting sexual environment.

3. **Loyal and Devoted:** Loyalty is a hallmark of Cancer sexuality. They are deeply committed to their partners and strive to build stable and long-lasting relationships. This devotion translates into a strong desire to create meaningful and fulfilling sexual experiences.

4. **Sensual and Affectionate:** Cancer individuals have a heightened appreciation for physical touch and affection. They enjoy gentle, loving touches and often express their love and desire through cuddling, caressing, and other forms of physical affection.

5. **Protective and Security-Oriented:** Cancers value security and stability in their relationships. They seek to create a safe and secure environment for their partner, both emotionally and physically,

which allows them to fully express their sexuality without fear or inhibition.

Recommended Sex Toys and Practices for Cancer

Given their emotional and nurturing nature, Cancer individuals are best suited to sex toys and practices that emphasize intimacy, comfort, and emotional connection. Here are some top recommendations:

Sex Toys for Cancer:

1. **Luxury Vibrators:** High-quality vibrators made from soft, body-safe materials can provide gentle and soothing stimulation. Look for vibrators with multiple settings to customize the intensity and pattern of vibration to suit Cancer's sensitive nature.

2. **G-Spot Vibrators:** Designed to target the G-spot, these vibrators can provide deep and satisfying internal stimulation. The curved shape and gentle vibrations can help Cancer individuals explore their inner desires and experience intense pleasure.

3. **Clitoral Suction Toys:** These toys offer gentle, rhythmic suction that mimics the sensation of oral sex. The precise and luxurious stimulation can be deeply satisfying for Cancer individuals who enjoy slow and thorough pleasure.

4. **Body Massagers:** Full-body massagers that deliver soothing vibrations can enhance Cancer's appreciation for physical touch. These can be used for sensual massages that relax and arouse, creating a deeply intimate experience.

5. **Couples' Vibrators:** Designed to be worn during intercourse, couples' vibrators provide simultaneous stimulation for both partners. Cancer will appreciate the shared pleasure these toys offer, enhancing their connection with their partner.

6. **Soft Restraints:** For those Cancer individuals who enjoy a bit of kink, soft restraints made from plush materials like velvet or faux fur can add an element of excitement while still maintaining their need for comfort and safety.

Sexual Practices for Cancer:

1. **Sensual Massages:** Cancer individuals love physical touch and relaxation. Start with a full-body massage using warm, aromatic oils to awaken their senses and create a deeply relaxing and arousing atmosphere.
2. **Slow and Gentle Lovemaking:** Cancer prefers a slow and steady approach to sex. Focus on prolonged foreplay, gentle touches, and deep, rhythmic thrusts to build up intense pleasure gradually.
3. **Cuddling and Affection:** Physical affection is crucial for Cancer. Spend time cuddling, kissing, and caressing your Cancer partner to create a strong emotional bond and enhance their sexual experience.
4. **Intimate Conversations:** Cancer individuals value emotional connection and communication. Engage in intimate conversations, share your desires and fantasies, and create a safe space for emotional vulnerability.
5. **Bath or Shower Sex:** Share a warm bath or shower with your Cancer partner, using the water and soap to enhance your connection and create a soothing, intimate setting. This can be a deeply relaxing and sensual experience.
6. **Comfort and Safety:** Ensure the environment is comfortable and secure. Cancer individuals appreciate a stable and nurturing setting, so clean sheets, soft pillows, and a warm room can enhance their sexual experience.

Cancer and the Wiccan Wheel of the Year: Seasonal Sensuality

The Wiccan Wheel of the Year consists of eight seasonal festivals that celebrate the changing seasons and the natural rhythms of the Earth. Each festival carries its own unique energy, which can influence Cancer's sexual desires and experiences. Understanding these seasonal influences can help Cancer individuals and their partners enhance their connection and pleasure throughout the year.

The Wiccan Wheel of the Year:

1. **Samhain (October 31st - November 1st):** Samhain marks the end of the harvest and the beginning of winter. This festival is a time for reflection and honoring ancestors. For Cancer, it's an ideal time for deep emotional connection and intimate conversations. Engage in slow, sensual lovemaking that emphasizes emotional intimacy and bonding.

2. **Yule (December 20th - 23rd):** Yule celebrates the winter solstice and the return of the light. It's a time for warmth, comfort, and togetherness. Create a cozy and nurturing environment for your Cancer partner with warm blankets, soft lighting, and comforting touches. Focus on gentle and loving sexual experiences that emphasize security and affection.

3. **Imbolc (February 1st - 2nd):** Imbolc marks the beginning of spring and the awakening of new life. This festival is a time for renewal and growth. For Cancer, it's an opportunity to explore new aspects of their sexuality and try new experiences. Engage in playful and experimental sexual activities that bring excitement and freshness to your relationship.

4. **Ostara (March 20th - 23rd):** Ostara celebrates the spring equinox and the balance of light and dark. It's a time for fertility, growth, and new beginnings. Embrace the energy of Ostara by focusing on fertility and creativity in your sexual relationship. Engage in sensual and loving experiences that emphasize growth and connection.

5. **Beltane (April 30th - May 1st):** Beltane is a festival of fertility and passion, celebrating the height of spring. It's a time for exuberance and joy. For Cancer, it's an ideal time to indulge in passionate and playful sexual experiences. Engage in outdoor sex, playful teasing, and vibrant lovemaking that celebrates life and fertility.

6. **Litha (June 20th - 23rd):** Litha marks the summer solstice and the longest day of the year. It's a time for celebration, abundance, and joy. Create a festive and joyful environment for your Cancer partner with bright colors, fresh flowers, and uplifting music. Focus on joyful and celebratory sexual experiences that emphasize pleasure and abundance.

7. **Lammas (August 1st - 2nd):** Lammas celebrates the first harvest and the abundance of the Earth. It's a time for gratitude and celebration. For Cancer, it's an opportunity to focus on nurturing and giving. Engage in loving and nurturing sexual experiences that emphasize gratitude and appreciation for your partner.

8. **Mabon (September 20th - 23rd):** Mabon marks the autumn equinox and the balance of light and dark. It's a time for reflection and balance. Embrace the energy of Mabon by focusing on balance and harmony in your sexual relationship. Engage in balanced and harmonious sexual experiences that emphasize emotional and physical connection.

Conclusion

Cancer individuals, with their emotional and nurturing nature, thrive on intimacy, comfort, and emotional connection. By understanding their key sexual characteristics, selecting the right toys and practices, and aligning their intimate experiences with the Wiccan Wheel of the Year, Cancer can fully embrace their deeply emotional and nurturing nature and enjoy a fulfilling and satisfying sex life. The following chapters will continue to provide tailored advice for each zodiac sign, helping everyone discover the cosmic pleasures that align with their astrological profile.

Chapter 7: Leo - Confident and Dramatic
Sexual Characteristics of Leo

Leo, the fifth sign of the zodiac, is ruled by the Sun, the center of our solar system. As a fire sign, Leos are known for their confidence, charisma, and dramatic flair. These traits make them passionate and enthusiastic lovers who enjoy being the center of attention and bringing excitement and intensity to their sexual encounters.

Key Sexual Characteristics of Leo:

1. **Confident and Charismatic:** Leos exude confidence and charisma, which makes them highly attractive and magnetic. They enjoy taking the lead in the bedroom and are not afraid to express their desires and needs.
2. **Dramatic and Enthusiastic:** Leos love to put on a show and bring a sense of drama and excitement to their sexual encounters. They thrive on intensity and passion, making every experience memorable and exhilarating.
3. **Generous and Warm-Hearted:** Despite their desire for attention, Leos are generous lovers who take pleasure in satisfying their partners. They are attentive and affectionate, always striving to make their partner feel special and adored.
4. **Playful and Adventurous:** Leos enjoy fun and adventure in their sex life. They are open to trying new things and enjoy keeping their sexual experiences lively and varied.
5. **Proud and Dignified:** Leos have a strong sense of pride and dignity. They appreciate partners who admire and respect them, and they take great care in maintaining their appearance and performance in the bedroom.

Recommended Sex Toys and Practices for Leo

Given their confident and dramatic nature, Leo individuals are best suited to sex toys and practices that emphasize intensity, excitement, and a touch of luxury. Here are some top recommendations:

Sex Toys for Leo:

1. **Luxury Vibrators:** High-end vibrators made from premium materials such as medical-grade silicone or polished metal can appeal to Leo's love for luxury and sophistication. Look for vibrators with powerful motors and multiple settings to provide intense and customizable stimulation.

2. **Wand Massagers:** Known for their strong and rumbly vibrations, wand massagers can deliver deep, satisfying pleasure to Leos. They are perfect for external stimulation and can be used all over the body, adding an element of dramatic flair to their sexual experiences.

3. **Dual-Action Vibrators:** These vibrators offer simultaneous internal and external stimulation, providing intense and multi-faceted pleasure. Leos will appreciate the powerful sensations and the ability to explore multiple erogenous zones at once.

4. **Remote-Controlled Toys:** Toys that can be controlled remotely via a wireless remote or smartphone app add an element of surprise and excitement. Leos can enjoy the thrill of unexpected pleasure, whether at home or in public settings.

5. **Nipple Clamps:** For Leos who enjoy a bit of kink, nipple clamps can provide a combination of pain and pleasure. The sensation of the clamps can be both arousing and exciting, adding a dramatic touch to their sexual play.

6. **Body Chains and Jewelry:** Erotic body chains and jewelry can add a touch of glamour and sophistication to Leo's sexual experiences. These accessories can enhance their appearance and make them feel even more confident and admired.

Sexual Practices for Leo:

1. **Role-Playing and Fantasy:** Leos' love for drama and performance makes role-playing an exciting and stimulating practice. Whether it's dressing up in costumes or acting out fantasies, role-playing allows Leos to explore different personas and scenarios.

2. **Public Displays of Affection:** Leos enjoy being the center of attention, and public displays of affection can be a thrilling way to express their passion. From kissing in public to engaging in discreet public play, Leos can indulge in their love for drama and excitement.

3. **Intense and Passionate Lovemaking:** Leos thrive on intensity and passion. Engage in vigorous and enthusiastic lovemaking that allows Leos to fully express their energy and desires. Positions that involve deep thrusting and active participation, such as doggy style or standing sex, can be particularly enjoyable.

4. **Erotic Dancing:** Leos love to put on a show, and erotic dancing can be a fun and arousing way to set the mood. Whether it's a sensual striptease or a dramatic dance routine, Leos can use their confidence and charisma to captivate their partner.

5. **Luxury and Comfort:** Create a luxurious and comfortable environment for your Leo partner with soft sheets, plush pillows, and ambient lighting. Leos appreciate the finer things in life, and a touch of luxury can enhance their sexual experience.

6. **Affirmation and Praise:** Leos thrive on admiration and praise. Make sure to compliment their appearance, performance, and efforts in the bedroom. This positive reinforcement will boost their confidence and enhance their pleasure.

Leo and Cosmic Events: Unleashing Passion

Cosmic events, such as planetary alignments, moon phases, and solar or lunar eclipses, can have a significant impact on Leo's sexual energy and experiences. Understanding these celestial influences can help Leo individuals and their partners unleash their passion and enhance their connection.

Moon Phases:

1. **New Moon:** The new moon represents new beginnings and is an excellent time for Leos to explore new sexual adventures or try out new toys. Setting intentions for your sex life during this phase can lead to exciting and fulfilling experiences.
2. **Full Moon:** The full moon amplifies emotions and desires, making it a potent time for intense and passionate encounters. Leos can use this energy to deepen their sexual connection with their partner, indulging in their wildest fantasies.
3. **Waxing Moon:** As the moon grows, so does energy and anticipation. This is a great time for Leos to build up sexual tension and excitement through prolonged foreplay and teasing, leading up to an explosive climax around the full moon.
4. **Waning Moon:** As the moon decreases, energy might wane slightly, making it a good time for Leos to focus on more intimate and nurturing sexual activities. This phase is ideal for connecting on a deeper emotional level with your partner.

Planetary Alignments:

1. **Sun Transits:** Since the Sun is Leo's ruling planet, its transits can significantly boost Leo's sexual energy. When the Sun is in a favorable position, Leos may feel more confident, radiant, and eager to pursue their desires.
   - **Example:** During Leo season (when the Sun is in Leo), Leos can experience heightened sexual energy and a strong desire to express their passions. This period is ideal for exploring new sexual activities and celebrating their sexuality.
2. **Mars Transits:** Mars influences passion and drive, and its transits can enhance Leo's sexual energy and desire. When Mars is in

a favorable position, Leos may feel more assertive and eager to pursue their sexual desires.

- ◦ **Example:** During a Mars sextile with the Sun, Leos can experience heightened sexual energy and a strong sense of confidence. This alignment can be an ideal time for exploring new sexual activities and expressing their desires with enthusiasm.

3. **Venus Alignments:** Alignments involving Venus can enhance Leo's romantic and sensual inclinations. This is an ideal time for Leos to focus on pleasure, beauty, and love, indulging in luxurious and sensual experiences.

- ◦ **Example:** When Venus forms a trine with the Sun, Leos can experience a harmonious blend of romance and passion. This alignment can lead to deep, meaningful connections and intensely pleasurable sexual experiences.

4. **Jupiter Transits:** Jupiter's expansive energy can encourage Leos to explore new horizons in their sexual life. Alignments involving Jupiter can bring a sense of adventure and optimism, making it a perfect time for trying new things.

- ◦ **Example:** When Jupiter forms a conjunction with the Sun, Leos can feel an increased sense of confidence and a desire for growth. This alignment can lead to the exploration of new sexual techniques, toys, or practices.

Conclusion

Leo individuals, with their confident and dramatic nature, thrive on intensity, excitement, and a touch of luxury. By understanding their key sexual characteristics, selecting the right toys and practices, and aligning their intimate experiences with cosmic events, Leos can fully embrace their passionate and charismatic nature and enjoy a fulfilling and dynamic sex life. The following chapters will continue to provide tailored advice for each zodiac sign, helping everyone discover the cosmic pleasures that align with their astrological profile.

Chapter 8: Virgo - Discreet and Meticulous
Sexual Characteristics of Virgo

Virgo, the sixth sign of the zodiac, is ruled by Mercury, the planet of communication and intellect. As an earth sign, Virgo individuals are known for their practicality, meticulousness, and attention to detail. These traits extend into their sexual lives, making them thoughtful and attentive lovers who prioritize quality over quantity and strive for perfection in their intimate experiences.

Key Sexual Characteristics of Virgo:

1. **Discreet and Private:** Virgos value their privacy and often approach their sexuality with discretion. They prefer intimate settings where they can feel safe and comfortable, away from prying eyes and distractions.
2. **Meticulous and Detail-Oriented:** Virgos are known for their meticulous nature and attention to detail. They bring this same level of care to their sexual encounters, ensuring that every aspect is carefully considered and executed to perfection.
3. **Thoughtful and Attentive:** Virgos are thoughtful lovers who take the time to understand their partner's needs and desires. They are highly attentive and focused on providing pleasure, often going above and beyond to ensure their partner is satisfied.
4. **Intellectual and Communicative:** Ruled by Mercury, Virgos value intellectual stimulation and clear communication. They enjoy discussing their desires and fantasies with their partner and appreciate a mental connection as much as a physical one.
5. **Practical and Grounded:** Virgos have a practical approach to life and this extends to their sexuality. They appreciate functionality and efficiency, and prefer straightforward, no-nonsense sexual experiences that are deeply satisfying.

Recommended Sex Toys and Practices for Virgo

Given their discreet and meticulous nature, Virgo individuals are best suited to sex toys and practices that emphasize precision, quality, and thoughtful attention to detail. Here are some top recommendations:

Sex Toys for Virgo:

1. **High-Quality Vibrators:** Virgos appreciate quality and precision, so high-end vibrators made from body-safe materials such as medical-grade silicone or polished metal are ideal. Look for vibrators with multiple settings that allow for precise control over intensity and pattern.

2. **G-Spot Vibrators:** Designed to target the G-spot, these vibrators can provide deep and satisfying internal stimulation. The curved shape and precise vibrations can help Virgo individuals explore their inner desires and experience intense pleasure.

3. **Clitoral Suction Toys:** These toys offer gentle, rhythmic suction that mimics the sensation of oral sex. The precise and luxurious stimulation can be deeply satisfying for Virgo individuals who enjoy slow and thorough pleasure.

4. **Anal Toys:** For Virgo individuals open to exploring anal play, anal plugs and beads offer a new dimension of pleasure. Their meticulous nature makes them eager to experiment with different sensations and experiences, ensuring every detail is considered.

5. **Remote-Controlled Toys:** Toys that can be controlled remotely via a wireless remote or smartphone app add an element of surprise and excitement. Virgos can enjoy the thrill of unexpected pleasure, whether at home or in public settings.

6. **Massage Wands:** Known for their strong and rumbly vibrations, massage wands can deliver deep, satisfying pleasure to Virgos. They are perfect for external stimulation and can be used all over the body, adding an element of relaxation and indulgence.

Sexual Practices for Virgo:

1. **Sensual Massages:** Virgos love physical touch and relaxation. Start with a full-body massage using warm, aromatic oils to awaken their senses and create a deeply relaxing and arousing atmosphere.

2. **Slow and Methodical Lovemaking:** Virgos prefer a slow and steady approach to sex. Focus on prolonged foreplay, gentle touches, and deep, rhythmic thrusts to build up intense pleasure gradually.

3. **Intimate Conversations:** Virgos value intellectual stimulation and clear communication. Engage in intimate conversations, share your desires and fantasies, and create a safe space for emotional vulnerability.

4. **Clean and Organized Environment:** Ensure the environment is clean and organized. Virgos appreciate a tidy and well-maintained setting, so clean sheets, soft pillows, and a fresh, inviting room can enhance their sexual experience.

5. **Precision and Technique:** Virgos appreciate precision and technique. Focus on perfecting your sexual techniques and paying attention to every detail to ensure a deeply satisfying experience for both partners.

6. **Aftercare and Nurturing:** Virgos are thoughtful and attentive lovers. Aftercare is important to them, so spend time cuddling, talking, and nurturing your partner after sex to create a strong emotional bond.

Virgo and Moon Phases: Precision in Pleasure

Moon phases can significantly influence Virgo's sexual energy and approach to intimacy. Understanding these phases can help Virgo individuals and their partners enhance their connection and pleasure.

Moon Phases:

1. **New Moon:** The new moon represents new beginnings and introspection. For Virgo, this phase is ideal for setting intentions

and exploring new aspects of their sexuality in a safe and private environment. Use this time to discuss desires and fantasies with your partner, setting the stage for future intimate experiences.

2. **Waxing Crescent:** As the moon begins to grow, so does energy and anticipation. This is a good time for Virgo to gradually build up intimacy and excitement. Focus on extended foreplay and gentle exploration, laying the groundwork for deeper connection.

3. **First Quarter:** The first quarter moon is a time of action and decision-making. Virgo can use this phase to actively pursue their sexual desires and take the initiative in their intimate relationships. Plan a special date night or surprise your partner with a sensual massage or a new sex toy.

4. **Waxing Gibbous:** As the moon approaches fullness, sexual energy and emotions intensify. Virgo can use this phase to deepen their connection through passionate and indulgent lovemaking. Experiment with different sensory elements and luxurious settings to enhance pleasure.

5. **Full Moon:** The full moon amplifies emotions and desires, making it a potent time for intense and passionate encounters. Virgo can fully embrace their meticulous nature, indulging in their wildest fantasies and exploring new levels of pleasure with their partner.

6. **Waning Gibbous:** As the moon begins to wane, energy levels start to decrease. This is a good time for Virgo to focus on nurturing and comforting activities. Engage in slow and tender lovemaking, emphasizing emotional connection and intimacy.

7. **Last Quarter:** The last quarter moon is a time for reflection and evaluation. Virgo can use this phase to reflect on their sexual experiences, discussing what worked well and what could be improved. This is also a good time to reinforce the emotional bond with their partner.

8. **Waning Crescent:** As the moon approaches the new phase, energy is low and introspection is high. Virgo can use this time for

rest and rejuvenation, focusing on self-care and gentle, intimate activities that promote relaxation and connection.

Conclusion

Virgo individuals, with their discreet and meticulous nature, thrive on precision, quality, and thoughtful attention to detail. By understanding their key sexual characteristics, selecting the right toys and practices, and aligning their intimate experiences with the moon phases, Virgos can fully embrace their deeply attentive and methodical nature and enjoy a fulfilling and satisfying sex life. The following chapters will continue to provide tailored advice for each zodiac sign, helping everyone discover the cosmic pleasures that align with their astrological profile

Chapter 9: Libra - Romantic and Balanced
Sexual Characteristics of Libra

Libra, the seventh sign of the zodiac, is ruled by Venus, the planet of love, beauty, and harmony. As an air sign, Libra individuals are known for their romantic nature, charm, and desire for balance and fairness in all aspects of life, including their sexual relationships. These traits make them passionate and considerate lovers who prioritize mutual satisfaction and aesthetic pleasure.

Key Sexual Characteristics of Libra:

1. **Romantic and Affectionate:** Libras are natural romantics who enjoy creating beautiful and loving environments for their partners. They thrive on affection, tenderness, and the art of seduction, making every sexual encounter feel like a fairy tale.

2. **Balanced and Fair:** Libras value equality and fairness in their relationships. They strive to ensure that both partners are equally satisfied and enjoy a balanced dynamic where mutual pleasure is prioritized.

3. **Charming and Diplomatic:** Libras are known for their charm and diplomacy. They excel in communication and use their skills to express their desires and understand their partner's needs, creating a harmonious and fulfilling sexual connection.

4. **Aesthetic and Sensual:** Ruled by Venus, Libras have a heightened appreciation for beauty and sensuality. They enjoy incorporating elements of luxury and aesthetics into their sexual experiences, such as candlelit settings, soft music, and elegant lingerie.

5. **Indecisive and Adaptable:** While Libras may sometimes struggle with decision-making, their adaptability makes them open to exploring different sexual preferences and practices. They are willing to try new things to ensure both partners are satisfied.

Recommended Sex Toys and Practices for Libra

Given their romantic and balanced nature, Libra individuals are best suited to sex toys and practices that emphasize mutual pleasure, beauty, and a touch of luxury. Here are some top recommendations:

Sex Toys for Libra:

1. **Couples' Vibrators:** Designed to be worn during intercourse, couples' vibrators provide simultaneous stimulation for both partners. Libras will appreciate the shared pleasure these toys offer, enhancing their connection and mutual satisfaction.

2. **Luxury Vibrators:** High-quality vibrators made from premium materials such as medical-grade silicone or polished metal can appeal to Libra's love for beauty and sophistication. Look for vibrators with multiple settings that allow for customized and harmonious stimulation.

3. **Bullet Vibrators:** Compact and versatile, bullet vibrators are perfect for precise and targeted stimulation. Libras can use these toys to enhance foreplay and create a sensual and romantic atmosphere.

4. **Body Massagers:** Full-body massagers that deliver soothing vibrations can enhance Libra's appreciation for physical touch and relaxation. These can be used for sensual massages that relax and arouse, creating a deeply intimate experience.

5. **Remote-Controlled Toys:** Toys that can be controlled remotely via a wireless remote or smartphone app add an element of surprise and excitement. Libras can enjoy the thrill of unexpected pleasure, whether at home or in public settings.

6. **Erotic Jewelry:** Body chains, nipple clamps, and other erotic jewelry can add a touch of elegance and sophistication to Libra's sexual experiences. These accessories can enhance their appearance and make them feel even more confident and admired.

Sexual Practices for Libra:

1. **Sensual Massages:** Libras love physical touch and relaxation. Start with a full-body massage using warm, aromatic oils to awaken their senses and create a deeply relaxing and arousing atmosphere.

2. **Slow and Gentle Lovemaking:** Libras prefer a slow and steady approach to sex. Focus on prolonged foreplay, gentle touches, and deep, rhythmic thrusts to build up intense pleasure gradually.

3. **Romantic Settings:** Create a beautiful and romantic environment for your Libra partner with soft lighting, scented candles, and luxurious bedding. Libras appreciate aesthetics and will feel more relaxed and aroused in a visually pleasing setting.

4. **Intimate Conversations:** Libras value intellectual and emotional connection. Engage in intimate conversations, share your desires and fantasies, and create a safe space for emotional vulnerability.

5. **Mutual Pleasure:** Ensure that both partners are equally satisfied by paying attention to each other's needs and desires. Libras thrive on balance and fairness, so mutual pleasure is essential for a fulfilling sexual experience.

6. **Role-Playing and Fantasy:** Libras' romantic nature makes role-playing an exciting and stimulating practice. Whether it's dressing up in costumes or acting out fantasies, role-playing allows Libras to explore different personas and scenarios.

Libra and Planet Alignments: Finding Harmony

Planetary alignments can significantly influence Libra's sexual energy and experiences. Understanding these alignments can help Libra individuals and their partners find harmony and enhance their connection.

Planetary Alignments:

1. **Venus Transits:** As Libra's ruling planet, Venus's transits have a strong impact on their sexual energy. When Venus is in a favorable position, Libras may feel more romantic, affectionate, and eager to pursue their desires.

- **Example:** During a Venus sextile with Mars, Libras can experience heightened sexual energy and a strong sense of passion. This alignment can be an ideal time for exploring new sexual activities and expressing their desires with enthusiasm.

2. **Mercury Transits:** Mercury influences communication and intellect, and its transits can enhance Libra's ability to express their desires and understand their partner's needs. Clear communication is essential for creating a harmonious sexual connection.

   - **Example:** During a Mercury trine with Venus, Libras can experience a harmonious blend of intellectual and physical attraction. This alignment can lead to deep, meaningful conversations that enhance their emotional and sexual connection.

3. **Mars Transits:** Mars influences passion and drive, and its transits can boost Libra's sexual energy and desire. When Mars is in a favorable position, Libras may feel more assertive and eager to pursue their sexual desires.

   - **Example:** During a Mars sextile with the Sun, Libras can experience heightened sexual energy and a strong sense of confidence. This alignment can be an ideal time for exploring new sexual activities and expressing their desires with enthusiasm.

4. **Jupiter Transits:** Jupiter's expansive energy can encourage Libras to explore new horizons in their sexual life. Alignments involving Jupiter can bring a sense of adventure and optimism, making it a perfect time for trying new things.

   - **Example:** When Jupiter forms a conjunction with Venus, Libras can feel an increased sense of confidence and a desire for growth. This alignment can lead to the exploration of new sexual techniques, toys, or practices.

Conclusion

Libra individuals, with their romantic and balanced nature, thrive on mutual pleasure, beauty, and a touch of luxury. By understanding their key sexual characteristics, selecting the right toys and practices, and aligning their intimate experiences with planetary alignments, Libras can fully embrace their passionate and harmonious nature and enjoy a fulfilling and dynamic sex life. The following chapters will continue to provide tailored advice for each zodiac sign, helping everyone discover the cosmic pleasures that align with their astrological profile.

Chapter 10: Scorpio - Intense and Passionate
Sexual Characteristics of Scorpio

Scorpio, the eighth sign of the zodiac, is ruled by both Mars and Pluto, planets associated with passion, transformation, and power. As a water sign, Scorpio individuals are known for their emotional depth, intensity, and magnetic allure. These traits make them deeply passionate and highly sexual beings who crave profound connections and transformative experiences in their intimate lives.

Key Sexual Characteristics of Scorpio:

1. **Intense and Passionate:** Scorpios are known for their intense and all-consuming passion. They approach their sexual relationships with a powerful desire to connect on a deep, emotional level, making every encounter incredibly meaningful.

2. **Magnetic and Alluring:** Scorpios have a natural magnetism and allure that draws people in. Their mysterious and seductive nature makes them irresistible, creating a strong and captivating sexual presence.

3. **Emotionally Deep:** Scorpios crave emotional depth and intimacy. They seek to understand their partner on the most profound levels, creating a bond that is both emotionally and sexually fulfilling.

4. **Transformative and Powerful:** Ruled by Pluto, the planet of transformation, Scorpios view sex as a powerful and transformative experience. They are not afraid to explore the darker, more intense aspects of sexuality, seeking to evolve and grow through their intimate connections.

5. **Secretive and Private:** Scorpios value their privacy and approach their sexuality with discretion. They prefer intimate settings where they can fully express their desires without fear of judgment or exposure.

Recommended Sex Toys and Practices for Scorpio

Given their intense and passionate nature, Scorpio individuals are best suited to sex toys and practices that emphasize depth, transformation, and powerful sensations. Here are some top recommendations:

Sex Toys for Scorpio:

1. **G-Spot and Prostate Vibrators:** Designed to target the G-spot in women and the prostate (or P-spot) in men, these vibrators provide deep and satisfying internal stimulation. The intense and precise vibrations can help Scorpios explore their inner desires and experience profound pleasure.

2. **Luxury Wand Massagers:** Known for their strong and rumbly vibrations, wand massagers can deliver deep, satisfying pleasure to Scorpios. They are perfect for external stimulation and can be used all over the body, adding an element of indulgence and power to their sexual experiences.

3. **Anal Toys:** For Scorpios open to exploring anal play, anal plugs, beads, and prostate massagers offer a new dimension of pleasure. Their adventurous nature makes them eager to experiment with different sensations and experiences, ensuring every detail is considered.

4. **Remote-Controlled and App-Enabled Toys:** Toys that can be controlled remotely via a wireless remote or smartphone app add an element of surprise and excitement. Scorpios can enjoy the thrill of unexpected pleasure, whether at home or in public settings.

5. **Bondage and BDSM Gear:** For Scorpios who enjoy exploring power dynamics and the transformative aspects of sexuality,

bondage gear such as cuffs, ropes, blindfolds, and gags can add an element of control and surrender, intensifying their sexual encounters.

6. **Nipple Clamps and Suction Toys:** These toys can provide a combination of pain and pleasure, adding a layer of intensity to Scorpio's sexual play. The sensation of the clamps or suction can be both arousing and exciting, aligning with their desire for powerful and transformative experiences.

Sexual Practices for Scorpio:

1. **Tantric Sex:** Tantric sex focuses on deep connection and prolonged pleasure. Scorpios can benefit from the slow, mindful approach of tantra, which emphasizes breathing, eye contact, and synchronization with their partner, creating a profound and transformative experience.

2. **Role-Playing and Fantasy:** Scorpios' love for intensity and transformation makes role-playing an exciting and stimulating practice. Whether it's dressing up in costumes or acting out fantasies, role-playing allows Scorpios to explore different personas and scenarios.

3. **Power Play:** Engage in power dynamics and BDSM practices that align with Scorpio's desire for control and surrender. This can include dominance and submission, bondage, impact play, and sensory deprivation, all conducted in a safe and consensual manner.

4. **Sensual Massages:** Scorpios love physical touch and relaxation. Start with a full-body massage using warm, aromatic oils to awaken their senses and create a deeply relaxing and arousing atmosphere.

5. **Deep Emotional Connection:** Scorpios thrive on emotional depth and intimacy. Engage in intimate conversations, share your

desires and fantasies, and create a safe space for emotional vulnerability to enhance the sexual experience.

6. **Intense and Passionate Lovemaking:** Scorpios prefer intense and passionate sex. Focus on deep, rhythmic thrusts, strong embraces, and prolonged eye contact to build up intense pleasure and emotional connection.

Scorpio and the Wiccan Wheel of the Year: Transforming Desire

The Wiccan Wheel of the Year consists of eight seasonal festivals that celebrate the changing seasons and the natural rhythms of the Earth. Each festival carries its own unique energy, which can influence Scorpio's sexual desires and experiences. Understanding these seasonal influences can help Scorpio individuals and their partners enhance their connection and pleasure throughout the year.

The Wiccan Wheel of the Year:

1. **Samhain (October 31st - November 1st):** Samhain marks the end of the harvest and the beginning of winter. This festival is a time for reflection and honoring ancestors. For Scorpio, it's an ideal time for deep emotional connection and intimate conversations. Engage in slow, sensual lovemaking that emphasizes emotional intimacy and bonding.

2. **Yule (December 20th - 23rd):** Yule celebrates the winter solstice and the return of the light. It's a time for warmth, comfort, and togetherness. Create a cozy and nurturing environment for your Scorpio partner with warm blankets, soft lighting, and comforting touches. Focus on gentle and loving sexual experiences that emphasize security and affection.

3. **Imbolc (February 1st - 2nd):** Imbolc marks the beginning of spring and the awakening of new life. This festival is a time for renewal and growth. For Scorpio, it's an opportunity to explore new aspects of their sexuality and try new experiences. Engage in

playful and experimental sexual activities that bring excitement and freshness to your relationship.

4. **Ostara (March 20th - 23rd):** Ostara celebrates the spring equinox and the balance of light and dark. It's a time for fertility, growth, and new beginnings. Embrace the energy of Ostara by focusing on fertility and creativity in your sexual relationship. Engage in sensual and loving experiences that emphasize growth and connection.

5. **Beltane (April 30th - May 1st):** Beltane is a festival of fertility and passion, celebrating the height of spring. It's a time for exuberance and joy. For Scorpio, it's an ideal time to indulge in passionate and playful sexual experiences. Engage in outdoor sex, playful teasing, and vibrant lovemaking that celebrates life and fertility.

6. **Litha (June 20th - 23rd):** Litha marks the summer solstice and the longest day of the year. It's a time for celebration, abundance, and joy. Create a festive and joyful environment for your Scorpio partner with bright colors, fresh flowers, and uplifting music. Focus on joyful and celebratory sexual experiences that emphasize pleasure and abundance.

7. **Lammas (August 1st - 2nd):** Lammas celebrates the first harvest and the abundance of the Earth. It's a time for gratitude and celebration. For Scorpio, it's an opportunity to focus on nurturing and giving. Engage in loving and nurturing sexual experiences that emphasize gratitude and appreciation for your partner.

8. **Mabon (September 20th - 23rd):** Mabon marks the autumn equinox and the balance of light and dark. It's a time for reflection and balance. Embrace the energy of Mabon by focusing on balance and harmony in your sexual relationship. Engage in balanced and harmonious sexual experiences that emphasize emotional and physical connection.

Conclusion

Scorpio individuals, with their intense and passionate nature, thrive on depth, transformation, and powerful sensations. By understanding their key sexual characteristics, selecting the right toys and practices, and aligning their intimate experiences with the Wiccan Wheel of the Year, Scorpios can fully embrace their deeply emotional and transformative nature and enjoy a fulfilling and satisfying sex life. The following chapters will continue to provide tailored advice for each zodiac sign, helping everyone discover the cosmic pleasures that align with their astrological profile.

Chapter 11: Sagittarius - Adventurous and Free-Spirited Sexual Characteristics of Sagittarius

Sagittarius, the ninth sign of the zodiac, is ruled by Jupiter, the planet of expansion, adventure, and wisdom. As a fire sign, Sagittarius individuals are known for their adventurous spirit, free-spirited nature, and unquenchable curiosity. These traits make them passionate and enthusiastic lovers who crave excitement, novelty, and exploration in their intimate lives.

Key Sexual Characteristics of Sagittarius:

1. **Adventurous and Curious:** Sagittarians are natural explorers who are always eager to try new things and push boundaries. Their adventurous spirit extends to their sex lives, making them open to experimentation and new experiences.
2. **Free-Spirited and Independent:** Sagittarians value their freedom and independence. They enjoy sexual encounters that allow them to express their individuality and avoid feeling restricted or confined.
3. **Energetic and Enthusiastic:** Sagittarians bring high energy and enthusiasm to their sexual relationships. They approach sex with a sense of fun and excitement, making every encounter lively and exhilarating.
4. **Honest and Direct:** Sagittarians are known for their honesty and directness. They are open about their desires and preferences, and they appreciate partners who communicate clearly and honestly.
5. **Philosophical and Open-Minded:** Ruled by Jupiter, Sagittarians have a philosophical approach to life and sex. They are open-minded and willing to explore different perspectives and experiences, making them versatile and adaptable lovers.

Recommended Sex Toys and Practices for Sagittarius

Given their adventurous and free-spirited nature, Sagittarius individuals are best suited to sex toys and practices that emphasize variety, novelty, and exploration. Here are some top recommendations:

Sex Toys for Sagittarius:

1. **Remote-Controlled and App-Enabled Toys:** Toys that can be controlled remotely via a wireless remote or smartphone app add an element of surprise and excitement. Sagittarians can enjoy the thrill of unexpected pleasure, whether at home or in public settings.

2. **Travel-Friendly Vibrators:** Compact and portable vibrators are perfect for Sagittarians who love to travel and explore new places. Look for discreet and versatile toys that can be easily packed and used on the go.

3. **Couples' Vibrators:** Designed to be worn during intercourse, couples' vibrators provide simultaneous stimulation for both partners. Sagittarians will appreciate the shared pleasure these toys offer, enhancing their connection and mutual satisfaction.

4. **Anal Toys:** For Sagittarians open to exploring anal play, anal plugs, beads, and prostate massagers offer a new dimension of pleasure. Their adventurous nature makes them eager to experiment with different sensations and experiences.

5. **Bondage and BDSM Gear:** For those Sagittarians who enjoy a bit of kink, bondage gear such as cuffs, ropes, blindfolds, and gags can add an element of excitement and exploration to their sexual play.

6. **Versatile Dildos:** Dildos that offer multiple uses, such as double-ended or strap-on options, can cater to Sagittarians' love for variety and novelty. These toys provide endless possibilities for experimentation and fun.

Sexual Practices for Sagittarius:

1. **Outdoor and Public Play:** The thrill of potential discovery can be a huge turn-on for Sagittarians. Engaging in sexual activities outdoors or in semi-public places can add a risky and exhilarating edge to their experiences.

2. **Role-Playing and Fantasy:** Sagittarians' love for adventure makes role-playing an exciting and stimulating practice. Whether it's dressing up in costumes or acting out fantasies, role-playing allows Sagittarians to explore different personas and scenarios.

3. **Spontaneous Sex:** Sagittarians thrive on spontaneity. Surprise your Sagittarius partner with unexpected intimate moments, whether it's a quickie in an unusual location or an impromptu seduction at home.

4. **Mutual Masturbation:** Watching and being watched can be highly arousing for Sagittarians. Mutual masturbation allows them to explore their own pleasure while simultaneously connecting with their partner.

5. **Sexual Games:** Incorporate playful competition and games into your sex life. From strip poker to sex dice, these activities cater to Sagittarians' love for fun and variety.

6. **Adventure and Exploration:** Plan sexual adventures that involve exploring new locations, trying new positions, or experimenting with new toys. Sagittarians will appreciate the novelty and excitement of these experiences.

Sagittarius and Cosmic Events: Exploring New Horizons

Cosmic events, such as planetary alignments, moon phases, and solar or lunar eclipses, can have a significant impact on Sagittarius's sexual energy and experiences. Understanding these celestial influences can help Sagittarius individuals and their partners explore new horizons and enhance their connection.

Moon Phases:

1. **New Moon:** The new moon represents new beginnings and is an excellent time for Sagittarians to explore new sexual adventures or try out new toys. Setting intentions for your sex life during this phase can lead to exciting and fulfilling experiences.

2. **Full Moon:** The full moon amplifies emotions and desires, making it a potent time for intense and passionate encounters. Sagittarians can use this energy to deepen their sexual connection with their partner, indulging in their wildest fantasies.

3. **Waxing Moon:** As the moon grows, so does energy and anticipation. This is a great time for Sagittarians to build up sexual tension and excitement through prolonged foreplay and teasing, leading up to an explosive climax around the full moon.

4. **Waning Moon:** As the moon decreases, energy might wane slightly, making it a good time for Sagittarians to focus on more intimate and nurturing sexual activities. This phase is ideal for connecting on a deeper emotional level with your partner.

Planetary Alignments:

1. **Jupiter Transits:** As Sagittarius's ruling planet, Jupiter's transits have a strong impact on their sexual energy. When Jupiter is in a favorable position, Sagittarians may feel more adventurous, optimistic, and eager to explore their desires.
   - **Example:** During a Jupiter sextile with Venus, Sagittarians can experience heightened sexual energy and a strong sense of passion. This alignment can be an ideal time for exploring new sexual activities and expressing their desires with enthusiasm.

2. **Mars Transits:** Mars influences passion and drive, and its transits can boost Sagittarius's sexual energy and desire. When Mars is in a favorable position, Sagittarians may feel more assertive and eager to pursue their sexual desires.

- **Example:** During a Mars sextile with Jupiter, Sagittarians can experience heightened sexual energy and a strong sense of confidence. This alignment can be an ideal time for exploring new sexual activities and expressing their desires with enthusiasm.

3. **Venus Alignments:** Alignments involving Venus can enhance Sagittarius's romantic and sensual inclinations. This is an ideal time for Sagittarians to focus on pleasure, beauty, and love, indulging in luxurious and sensual experiences.

   - **Example:** When Venus forms a trine with Jupiter, Sagittarians can experience a harmonious blend of romance and passion. This alignment can lead to deep, meaningful connections and intensely pleasurable sexual experiences.

4. **Eclipses:** Solar and lunar eclipses can bring about sudden changes and revelations. Sagittarians can use these powerful cosmic events to break free from sexual ruts and embrace transformative experiences that push their boundaries.

   - **Example:** During a lunar eclipse, Sagittarians can reflect on their sexual experiences and seek to transform their approach to intimacy. This period can be an opportunity for introspection and growth in their sexual relationships.

Conclusion

Sagittarius individuals, with their adventurous and free-spirited nature, thrive on variety, novelty, and exploration. By understanding their key sexual characteristics, selecting the right toys and practices, and aligning their intimate experiences with cosmic events, Sagittarians can fully embrace their passionate and dynamic nature and enjoy a fulfilling and adventurous sex life. The following chapters will continue to provide tailored advice for each zodiac sign, helping everyone discover the cosmic pleasures that align with their astrological profile.

Chapter 12: Capricorn - Disciplined and Ambitious
Sexual Characteristics of Capricorn

Capricorn, the tenth sign of the zodiac, is ruled by Saturn, the planet of discipline, responsibility, and structure. As an earth sign, Capricorns are known for their ambitious nature, practicality, and determination. These traits extend into their sexual lives, making them disciplined and goal-oriented lovers who prioritize quality and long-term fulfillment over short-term pleasure.

Key Sexual Characteristics of Capricorn:

1. **Disciplined and Patient:** Capricorns are known for their self-discipline and patience. They approach their sexual relationships with a focus on long-term satisfaction, taking the time to build a deep and meaningful connection with their partner.

2. **Ambitious and Goal-Oriented:** Capricorns are driven by their ambitions and strive for success in all aspects of life, including their sex lives. They set high standards for themselves and their partners, constantly seeking to improve and achieve greater levels of pleasure.

3. **Practical and Grounded:** Capricorns have a practical approach to life and sex. They value reliability and consistency, preferring straightforward and no-nonsense sexual experiences that are deeply satisfying and fulfilling.

4. **Loyal and Committed:** Capricorns are deeply loyal and committed to their partners. They prioritize building a stable and secure relationship, ensuring that their partner feels valued and appreciated.

5. **Reserved and Private:** Capricorns value their privacy and may initially appear reserved in their sexual relationships. However,

once they feel secure and comfortable, they are capable of deep emotional and physical intimacy.

Recommended Sex Toys and Practices for Capricorn

Given their disciplined and ambitious nature, Capricorn individuals are best suited to sex toys and practices that emphasize quality, practicality, and long-term fulfillment. Here are some top recommendations:

Sex Toys for Capricorn:

1. **High-Quality Vibrators:** Capricorns appreciate quality and precision, so high-end vibrators made from body-safe materials such as medical-grade silicone or polished metal are ideal. Look for vibrators with multiple settings that allow for precise control over intensity and pattern.

2. **G-Spot and Prostate Massagers:** Designed to target the G-spot in women and the prostate (or P-spot) in men, these massagers provide deep and satisfying internal stimulation. The intense and precise vibrations can help Capricorns explore their inner desires and achieve profound pleasure.

3. **Remote-Controlled and App-Enabled Toys:** Toys that can be controlled remotely via a wireless remote or smartphone app add an element of surprise and excitement. Capricorns can enjoy the thrill of unexpected pleasure, whether at home or in public settings.

4. **Bondage and BDSM Gear:** For Capricorns who enjoy exploring power dynamics and the disciplined aspects of sexuality, bondage gear such as cuffs, ropes, blindfolds, and gags can add an element of control and surrender, intensifying their sexual encounters.

5. **Weighted Kegel Balls:** For Capricorn women, weighted kegel balls can enhance pelvic floor strength and increase sexual pleasure. The sensation of the weights can be both arousing and beneficial for sexual health.

6. **Luxury Dildos:** Dildos that offer multiple uses, such as double-ended or strap-on options, can cater to Capricorns' love for variety and novelty. These toys provide endless possibilities for experimentation and long-term satisfaction.

Sexual Practices for Capricorn:

1. **Sensual Massages:** Capricorns love physical touch and relaxation. Start with a full-body massage using warm, aromatic oils to awaken their senses and create a deeply relaxing and arousing atmosphere.
2. **Slow and Methodical Lovemaking:** Capricorns prefer a slow and steady approach to sex. Focus on prolonged foreplay, gentle touches, and deep, rhythmic thrusts to build up intense pleasure gradually.
3. **Intimate Conversations:** Capricorns value intellectual and emotional connection. Engage in intimate conversations, share your desires and fantasies, and create a safe space for emotional vulnerability.
4. **Clean and Organized Environment:** Ensure the environment is clean and organized. Capricorns appreciate a tidy and well-maintained setting, so clean sheets, soft pillows, and a fresh, inviting room can enhance their sexual experience.
5. **Precision and Technique:** Capricorns appreciate precision and technique. Focus on perfecting your sexual techniques and paying attention to every detail to ensure a deeply satisfying experience for both partners.
6. **Aftercare and Nurturing:** Capricorns are thoughtful and attentive lovers. Aftercare is important to them, so spend time cuddling, talking, and nurturing your partner after sex to create a strong emotional bond.

Capricorn and Moon Phases: Achieving Fulfillment

Moon phases can significantly influence Capricorn's sexual energy and approach to intimacy. Understanding these phases can help Capricorn individuals and their partners achieve fulfillment and enhance their connection.

Moon Phases:

1. **New Moon:** The new moon represents new beginnings and introspection. For Capricorn, this phase is ideal for setting intentions and exploring new aspects of their sexuality in a safe and private environment. Use this time to discuss desires and fantasies with your partner, setting the stage for future intimate experiences.

2. **Waxing Crescent:** As the moon begins to grow, so does energy and anticipation. This is a good time for Capricorn to gradually build up intimacy and excitement. Focus on extended foreplay and gentle exploration, laying the groundwork for deeper connection.

3. **First Quarter:** The first quarter moon is a time of action and decision-making. Capricorns can use this phase to actively pursue their sexual desires and take the initiative in their intimate relationships. Plan a special date night or surprise your partner with a sensual massage or a new sex toy.

4. **Waxing Gibbous:** As the moon approaches fullness, sexual energy and emotions intensify. Capricorns can use this phase to deepen their connection through passionate and indulgent lovemaking. Experiment with different sensory elements and luxurious settings to enhance pleasure.

5. **Full Moon:** The full moon amplifies emotions and desires, making it a potent time for intense and passionate encounters. Capricorns can fully embrace their meticulous nature, indulging in their wildest fantasies and exploring new levels of pleasure with their partner.

6. **Waning Gibbous:** As the moon begins to wane, energy levels start to decrease. This is a good time for Capricorns to focus on

nurturing and comforting activities. Engage in slow and tender lovemaking, emphasizing emotional connection and intimacy.

7. **Last Quarter:** The last quarter moon is a time for reflection and evaluation. Capricorns can use this phase to reflect on their sexual experiences, discussing what worked well and what could be improved. This is also a good time to reinforce the emotional bond with their partner.

8. **Waning Crescent:** As the moon approaches the new phase, energy is low and introspection is high. Capricorns can use this time for rest and rejuvenation, focusing on self-care and gentle, intimate activities that promote relaxation and connection.

Conclusion

Capricorn individuals, with their disciplined and ambitious nature, thrive on quality, practicality, and long-term fulfillment. By understanding their key sexual characteristics, selecting the right toys and practices, and aligning their intimate experiences with the moon phases, Capricorns can fully embrace their deeply attentive and methodical nature and enjoy a fulfilling and satisfying sex life. The following chapters will continue to provide tailored advice for each zodiac sign, helping everyone discover the cosmic pleasures that align with their astrological profile.

Chapter 13: Aquarius - Innovative and Experimental
Sexual Characteristics of Aquarius

Aquarius, the eleventh sign of the zodiac, is ruled by Uranus, the planet of innovation, rebellion, and sudden change. As an air sign, Aquarius individuals are known for their intellectualism, unconventional thinking, and progressive attitudes. These traits make them highly innovative and experimental lovers who crave novelty, mental stimulation, and freedom in their intimate lives.

Key Sexual Characteristics of Aquarius:

1. **Innovative and Open-Minded:** Aquarians are naturally curious and always open to exploring new ideas and experiences. They are innovative in their approach to sex, constantly seeking new ways to enhance pleasure and intimacy.

2. **Experimental and Adventurous:** Aquarians thrive on experimentation and adventure. They enjoy pushing boundaries and trying out new techniques, positions, and toys, making their sexual encounters dynamic and exciting.

3. **Intellectual and Analytical:** Ruled by Uranus, Aquarians value intellectual stimulation as much as physical pleasure. They enjoy deep conversations, sharing fantasies, and understanding the psychology behind scxual desire.

4. **Independent and Unconventional:** Aquarians value their independence and often have unconventional views on relationships

and sexuality. They are open to non-traditional arrangements and prefer partners who respect their need for freedom and individuality.

5. **Humanitarian and Compassionate:** Despite their independent nature, Aquarians have a strong sense of compassion and humanitarianism. They seek to create meaningful connections and ensure that their partners feel valued and respected.

Recommended Sex Toys and Practices for Aquarius

Given their innovative and experimental nature, Aquarius individuals are best suited to sex toys and practices that emphasize novelty, mental stimulation, and freedom. Here are some top recommendations:

Sex Toys for Aquarius:

1. **App-Enabled and Remote-Controlled Toys:** Toys that can be controlled remotely via a smartphone app add an element of tech-savvy innovation and excitement. Aquarians can enjoy the thrill of unexpected pleasure and the ability to control their partner's toy from anywhere in the world.

2. **Versatile Vibrators:** Aquarians appreciate versatility and innovation in their sex toys. Look for vibrators that offer multiple functions, such as dual stimulation, customizable patterns, and various attachments that can be used in different ways.

3. **Kegel Exercisers:** For Aquarius women, high-tech Kegel exercisers that connect to apps can provide both physical and mental stimulation. These devices often include games or challenges that make strengthening the pelvic floor muscles fun and engaging.

4. **Electro-Stimulation Toys:** Aquarians' experimental nature makes them ideal candidates for electro-stimulation toys. These toys use mild electrical currents to provide unique sensations that can be both stimulating and arousing.

5. **Sex Swings and Position Enhancers:** To satisfy their adventurous spirit, Aquarians can benefit from sex swings and position

enhancers that allow for a variety of positions and angles, adding an element of novelty and excitement to their sexual experiences.

6. **Futuristic and High-Tech Toys:** Aquarians are drawn to cutting-edge technology and futuristic designs. Look for toys with sleek, modern aesthetics and advanced features that align with their innovative mindset.

Sexual Practices for Aquarius:

1. **Intellectual Foreplay:** Engage in deep and stimulating conversations with your Aquarius partner. Discuss fantasies, desires, and the psychology of sex to create a strong mental connection that enhances physical intimacy.

2. **Role-Playing and Fantasy:** Aquarians' love for innovation makes role-playing an exciting and stimulating practice. Whether it's dressing up in futuristic costumes or acting out unconventional fantasies, role-playing allows Aquarians to explore different personas and scenarios.

3. **Spontaneous and Adventurous Sex:** Aquarians thrive on spontaneity and adventure. Surprise your Aquarius partner with unexpected intimate moments, whether it's a quickie in an unusual location or an impromptu seduction at home.

4. **Non-Traditional Relationships:** Aquarians are open to exploring non-traditional relationship structures, such as open relationships or polyamory. Ensure open and honest communication to create a dynamic and fulfilling arrangement.

5. **Tech-Savvy Play:** Incorporate technology into your sex life by using app-enabled toys, watching VR porn, or engaging in long-distance control of toys. Aquarians will appreciate the innovative and futuristic aspects of tech-savvy play.

6. **Experimentation and Variety:** Constantly introduce new techniques, positions, and toys into your sexual repertoire. Aquarians

enjoy variety and experimentation, so keep things fresh and exciting to maintain their interest and enthusiasm.

Aquarius and Planet Alignments: Embracing Uniqueness

Planetary alignments can significantly influence Aquarius's sexual energy and experiences. Understanding these alignments can help Aquarius individuals and their partners embrace their uniqueness and enhance their connection.

Planetary Alignments:

1. **Uranus Transits:** As Aquarius's ruling planet, Uranus's transits have a strong impact on their sexual energy. When Uranus is in a favorable position, Aquarians may feel more innovative, adventurous, and eager to explore their desires.
   - **Example:** During a Uranus sextile with Venus, Aquarians can experience heightened sexual energy and a strong sense of excitement. This alignment can be an ideal time for exploring new sexual activities and expressing their desires with enthusiasm.

2. **Mercury Transits:** Mercury influences communication and intellect, and its transits can enhance Aquarius's ability to express their desires and understand their partner's needs. Clear communication is essential for creating a harmonious sexual connection.
   - **Example:** During a Mercury trine with Uranus, Aquarians can experience a harmonious blend of intellectual and physical attraction. This alignment can lead to deep, meaningful conversations that enhance their emotional and sexual connection.

3. **Mars Transits:** Mars influences passion and drive, and its transits can boost Aquarius's sexual energy and desire. When Mars is in a favorable position, Aquarians may feel more assertive and eager to pursue their sexual desires.

- ○ **Example:** During a Mars sextile with Uranus, Aquarians can experience heightened sexual energy and a strong sense of confidence. This alignment can be an ideal time for exploring new sexual activities and expressing their desires with enthusiasm.

4. **Venus Alignments:** Alignments involving Venus can enhance Aquarius's romantic and sensual inclinations. This is an ideal time for Aquarians to focus on pleasure, beauty, and love, indulging in luxurious and sensual experiences.

- ○ **Example:** When Venus forms a trine with Uranus, Aquarians can experience a harmonious blend of romance and passion. This alignment can lead to deep, meaningful connections and intensely pleasurable sexual experiences.

5. **Jupiter Transits:** Jupiter's expansive energy can encourage Aquarians to explore new horizons in their sexual life. Alignments involving Jupiter can bring a sense of adventure and optimism, making it a perfect time for trying new things.

- ○ **Example:** When Jupiter forms a conjunction with Uranus, Aquarians can feel an increased sense of confidence and a desire for growth. This alignment can lead to the exploration of new sexual techniques, toys, or practices.

Conclusion

Aquarius individuals, with their innovative and experimental nature, thrive on novelty, mental stimulation, and freedom. By understanding their key sexual characteristics, selecting the right toys and practices, and aligning their intimate experiences with planetary alignments, Aquarians can fully embrace their unique and dynamic nature and enjoy a fulfilling and adventurous sex life. The following chapters will continue to provide tailored advice for each zodiac sign, helping everyone discover the cosmic pleasures that align with their astrological profile.

Chapter 14: Pisces - Dreamy and Intuitive
Sexual Characteristics of Pisces

Pisces, the twelfth and final sign of the zodiac, is ruled by Neptune, the planet of dreams, intuition, and spiritual connection. As a water sign, Pisces individuals are known for their deep emotional sensitivity, creativity, and compassionate nature. These traits make them deeply intuitive and empathetic lovers who crave mystical and transcendental experiences in their intimate lives.

Key Sexual Characteristics of Pisces:

1. **Dreamy and Romantic:** Pisceans are natural romantics who thrive on creating beautiful, ethereal experiences for their partners. They are deeply imaginative and often approach sex as a form of artistic and emotional expression.

2. **Intuitive and Empathetic:** Pisces individuals have a heightened sense of intuition and empathy. They are highly attuned to their partner's emotions and desires, often knowing what their partner needs even before they do.

3. **Compassionate and Nurturing:** Pisceans are compassionate lovers who prioritize their partner's comfort and satisfaction. They derive immense pleasure from nurturing their partner and creating a safe, loving environment.

4. **Creative and Imaginative:** Ruled by Neptune, Pisces are incredibly creative and imaginative. They enjoy exploring fantasies and bringing a sense of wonder and magic to their sexual experiences.

5. **Spiritual and Transcendent:** Pisceans often view sex as a spiritual and transcendent experience. They seek to connect with their partner on a deeper, soul-level, creating intimate moments that feel mystical and profound.

Recommended Sex Toys and Practices for Pisces

Given their dreamy and intuitive nature, Pisces individuals are best suited to sex toys and practices that emphasize emotional connection, creativity, and transcendence. Here are some top recommendations:

Sex Toys for Pisces:

1. **Luxury Vibrators:** High-quality vibrators made from body-safe materials such as medical-grade silicone or polished metal are ideal for Pisces. Look for vibrators with multiple settings that allow for gentle and soothing stimulation, enhancing their romantic and dreamy nature.

2. **G-Spot and Clitoral Suction Toys:** Designed to target the G-spot and clitoris with precision, these toys can provide deep and satisfying internal and external stimulation. The gentle, rhythmic suction mimics the sensation of oral sex, adding an element of luxury and pleasure.

3. **Remote-Controlled and App-Enabled Toys:** Toys that can be controlled remotely via a smartphone app add an element of excitement and spontaneity. Pisces can enjoy the thrill of un-expected pleasure and the ability to connect with their partner from a distance.

4. **Waterproof Toys:** Pisceans' affinity for water makes waterproof toys an excellent choice. These toys can be used in the bath or shower, adding an element of relaxation and sensuality to their sexual experiences.

5. **Massage Wands:** Known for their strong and rumbly vibrations, massage wands can deliver deep, satisfying pleasure to Pisceans. They are perfect for external stimulation and can be used all over the body, creating a deeply relaxing and intimate experience.

6. **Erotic Accessories:** Feather ticklers, silk scarves, and scented candles can enhance the sensory experience for Pisces. These accessories add a touch of magic and creativity to their intimate moments, aligning with their imaginative and romantic nature.

Sexual Practices for Pisces:

1. **Sensual Massages:** Pisceans love physical touch and relaxation. Start with a full-body massage using warm, aromatic oils to awaken their senses and create a deeply relaxing and arousing atmosphere.

2. **Slow and Sensual Lovemaking:** Pisces prefer a slow and steady approach to sex. Focus on prolonged foreplay, gentle touches, and deep, rhythmic thrusts to build up intense pleasure gradually.

3. **Intimate Conversations:** Pisceans value emotional and spiritual connection. Engage in intimate conversations, share your desires and fantasies, and create a safe space for emotional vulnerability.

4. **Bath or Shower Sex:** Pisceans' affinity for water makes bath or shower sex a deeply satisfying experience. The warm water and soothing sensations can enhance their relaxation and arousal, creating a mystical and intimate setting.

5. **Role-Playing and Fantasy:** Pisceans' love for creativity and imagination makes role-playing an exciting and stimulating practice. Whether it's dressing up in costumes or acting out fantasies, role-playing allows Pisceans to explore different personas and scenarios.

6. **Meditative and Tantric Practices:** Incorporate meditative and tantric practices into your sex life. Focus on deep breathing, eye contact, and synchronization with your partner to create a spiritual and transcendent experience.

Pisces and the Wiccan Wheel of the Year: Mystical Experiences
The Wiccan Wheel of the Year consists of eight seasonal festivals that celebrate the changing seasons and the natural rhythms of the Earth. Each festival carries its own unique energy, which can influence Pisces's sexual desires and experiences. Understanding these seasonal influences can help Pisces individuals and their partners enhance their connection and pleasure throughout the year.

The Wiccan Wheel of the Year:

1. **Samhain (October 31st - November 1st):** Samhain marks the end of the harvest and the beginning of winter. This festival is a time for reflection and honoring ancestors. For Pisces, it's an ideal time for deep emotional connection and intimate conversations. Engage in slow, sensual lovemaking that emphasizes emotional intimacy and bonding.

2. **Yule (December 20th - 23rd):** Yule celebrates the winter solstice and the return of the light. It's a time for warmth, comfort, and togetherness. Create a cozy and nurturing environment for your Pisces partner with warm blankets, soft lighting, and comforting touches. Focus on gentle and loving sexual experiences that emphasize security and affection.

3. **Imbolc (February 1st - 2nd):** Imbolc marks the beginning of spring and the awakening of new life. This festival is a time for renewal and growth. For Pisces, it's an opportunity to explore new aspects of their sexuality and try new experiences. Engage in playful and experimental sexual activities that bring excitement and freshness to your relationship.

4. **Ostara (March 20th - 23rd):** Ostara celebrates the spring equinox and the balance of light and dark. It's a time for fertility, growth, and new beginnings. Embrace the energy of Ostara by focusing on fertility and creativity in your sexual relationship. Engage in sensual and loving experiences that emphasize growth and connection.

5. **Beltane (April 30th - May 1st):** Beltane is a festival of fertility and passion, celebrating the height of spring. It's a time for exuberance and joy. For Pisces, it's an ideal time to indulge in passionate and playful sexual experiences. Engage in outdoor sex, playful teasing, and vibrant lovemaking that celebrates life and fertility.

6. **Litha (June 20th - 23rd):** Litha marks the summer solstice and the longest day of the year. It's a time for celebration, abundance, and joy. Create a festive and joyful environment for your Pisces partner with bright colors, fresh flowers, and uplifting music. Focus on joyful and celebratory sexual experiences that emphasize pleasure and abundance.

7. **Lammas (August 1st - 2nd):** Lammas celebrates the first harvest and the abundance of the Earth. It's a time for gratitude and celebration. For Pisces, it's an opportunity to focus on nurturing and giving. Engage in loving and nurturing sexual experiences that emphasize gratitude and appreciation for your partner.

8. **Mabon (September 20th - 23rd):** Mabon marks the autumn equinox and the balance of light and dark. It's a time for reflection and balance. Embrace the energy of Mabon by focusing on balance and harmony in your sexual relationship. Engage in balanced and harmonious sexual experiences that emphasize emotional and physical connection.

Conclusion

Pisces individuals, with their dreamy and intuitive nature, thrive on emotional connection, creativity, and transcendence. By understanding their key sexual characteristics, selecting the right toys and practices, and aligning their intimate experiences with the Wiccan Wheel of the Year, Pisceans can fully embrace their deeply emotional and mystical nature and enjoy a fulfilling and satisfying sex life. The following chapters will continue to provide tailored advice for each zodiac sign, helping everyone discover the cosmic pleasures that align with their astrological profile.

Chapter 15: New Moon - Fresh Starts

Influence of the New Moon on Sexual Energy

The New Moon, a phase where the moon is not visible from Earth, marks the beginning of a new lunar cycle. This period symbolizes new beginnings, fresh starts, and the planting of seeds for future growth. Astrologically, the New Moon is a time of renewal, introspection, and setting intentions for the upcoming cycle. This energy profoundly influences our emotions, behaviors, and sexual dynamics.

Key Influences of the New Moon on Sexual Energy:

1. **Renewal and Rejuvenation:** The New Moon is a time for shedding old habits and embracing new perspectives. In terms of sexuality, it's an opportunity to let go of past disappointments or routines that no longer serve you and to open yourself up to new experiences and possibilities.

2. **Setting Intentions:** This phase is ideal for setting personal and relational goals. It's a perfect time to communicate with your partner about desires, fantasies, and sexual aspirations. Setting clear intentions can pave the way for more fulfilling and aligned sexual experiences.

3. **Introspection and Clarity:** The New Moon encourages introspection and self-awareness. Reflecting on your sexual needs, boundaries, and desires can lead to greater clarity and a deeper understanding of what truly satisfies you.

4. **New Beginnings:** The energy of the New Moon supports trying new things and stepping out of your comfort zone. It's an

excellent time to experiment with new toys, techniques, and practices that can invigorate your sex life and bring fresh excitement.

5. **Enhanced Intuition:** The New Moon heightens intuition and emotional sensitivity. This can enhance your ability to connect with your partner on a deeper emotional level, fostering a more intimate and empathetic sexual connection.

Recommended Toys and Practices for New Beginnings

Harnessing the energy of the New Moon can lead to transformative and enriching sexual experiences. Here are some recommended toys and practices that align with the theme of fresh starts and new beginnings:

Recommended Toys:

1. **Beginner's Vibrators:** For those new to sex toys or looking to start fresh, beginner's vibrators are a great choice. These toys are typically easy to use, non-intimidating, and provide a gentle introduction to the world of vibratory pleasure.
   - **Example:** A sleek, simple bullet vibrator or a small, discreet clitoral vibrator can offer precise stimulation and help explore new sensations.
2. **Couples' Kits:** Couples' kits often include a variety of toys designed for mutual pleasure and exploration. These kits can be a fun way to introduce new elements into your sex life and enhance intimacy with your partner.
   - **Example:** A kit that includes a vibrating cock ring, a small bullet vibrator, and a blindfold can add variety and excitement to your sexual repertoire.
3. **Remote-Controlled Toys:** Remote-controlled toys allow for playful and spontaneous interactions. These toys can be controlled by a partner, adding an element of surprise and anticipation to your sexual experiences.

- ◦ **Example:** A remote-controlled egg vibrator or a wearable panty vibrator can be a thrilling way to explore new dynamics in your relationship.

4. **Exploration Bundles:** These bundles often feature a selection of different types of toys, allowing you to experiment and discover what you enjoy most. They are perfect for those looking to try new things without committing to a single toy.
   - ◦ **Example:** A bundle that includes a variety of vibrators, dildos, and anal toys can provide a comprehensive introduction to different forms of pleasure.

5. **Intuitive Toys:** Toys designed to respond to your body's movements or touch can enhance the intuitive connection fostered by the New Moon's energy. These toys adapt to your rhythms, creating a more personalized experience.
   - ◦ **Example:** A touch-sensitive vibrator or a toy with motion-activated settings can provide a responsive and immersive experience.

Recommended Practices:

1. **Intentional Communication:** Use the New Moon's energy to have open and honest conversations with your partner about your sexual desires and boundaries. Setting intentions together can create a strong foundation for new and exciting experiences.
   - ◦ **Practice:** Have a "desire mapping" session where you and your partner discuss and list your sexual goals and fantasies. Use this as a guide to explore new areas of pleasure together.

2. **Exploration and Experimentation:** Embrace the spirit of new beginnings by trying out new toys, techniques, and positions. This is a time to step out of your comfort zone and discover new sources of pleasure.

- **Practice:** Plan an "adventure night" where you and your partner agree to try something completely new, whether it's a different position, a new toy, or a role-playing scenario.

3. **Sensual Rituals:** Incorporate rituals that align with the theme of renewal and intention-setting. These can help create a sacred and mindful approach to your sexual experiences.
   - **Practice:** Start with a cleansing bath or shower together, followed by lighting candles and setting your space with intention. Engage in a guided meditation or breathing exercise to connect on a deeper level before exploring each other's bodies.

4. **Solo Exploration:** The New Moon is also a powerful time for solo exploration and self-discovery. Use this period to understand your own body, desires, and boundaries better.
   - **Practice:** Dedicate an evening to self-pleasure, experimenting with different toys and techniques. Reflect on what feels good and what you might want to share with your partner.

5. **Mindful Masturbation:** Practice mindful masturbation, focusing on the sensations and your body's responses without rushing to orgasm. This can enhance your connection with your body and increase sexual awareness.
   - **Practice:** Use a gentle vibrator or your hands to explore your body slowly, paying attention to the different sensations and building up to orgasm gradually.

6. **Setting the Mood:** Create an environment that supports relaxation and intimacy. Soft lighting, calming music, and comfortable surroundings can enhance the experience and make it more meaningful.
   - **Practice:** Design a dedicated space for intimacy. This could be a special corner in your bedroom or a cozy spot in another part of your home where you feel safe and comfortable.

Conclusion

The New Moon, with its themes of renewal and fresh starts, offers a powerful opportunity to revitalize your sexual energy and explore new dimensions of pleasure. By understanding its influence, choosing the right toys, and adopting practices that align with this lunar phase, you can create deeply fulfilling and transformative sexual experiences. Embrace the New Moon's energy to set intentions, try new things, and deepen your connection with yourself and your partner. The following chapters will continue to explore the cosmic influences on sexuality, helping everyone discover the unique pleasures that align with their astrological profile.

Chapter 16: Waxing Crescent - Building Anticipation
Influence of the Waxing Crescent on Sexual Energy

The Waxing Crescent Moon follows the New Moon and marks the phase where the moon begins to grow and become more visible in the sky. This period symbolizes growth, potential, and the gradual build-up of energy. Astrologically, the Waxing Crescent is a time of increasing momentum, optimism, and anticipation. This energy profoundly influences our emotions, behaviors, and sexual dynamics.

Key Influences of the Waxing Crescent on Sexual Energy:

1. **Growth and Development:** The Waxing Crescent is a time for nurturing ideas and desires that were conceived during the New Moon. It's an ideal period for exploring new aspects of your sexuality and building on your intentions with your partner.

2. **Building Anticipation:** As the moon grows, so does the sense of anticipation and excitement. This phase is perfect for engaging in activities that build sexual tension and heighten desire, leading to a more fulfilling climax.

3. **Increasing Confidence:** The Waxing Crescent phase is associated with growing confidence and assertiveness. It's a time to express your desires more openly and take proactive steps toward achieving your sexual goals.

4. **Exploration and Experimentation:** The energy of this phase encourages exploration and experimentation. It's an excellent time to try new toys, techniques, and practices that can enhance your sexual experiences.

5. **Optimism and Excitement:** The Waxing Crescent brings a sense of optimism and excitement about the future. This positive

energy can invigorate your sex life, making it more vibrant and adventurous.

Recommended Toys and Practices for Anticipation

Harnessing the energy of the Waxing Crescent can lead to exhilarating and deeply satisfying sexual experiences. Here are some recommended toys and practices that align with the theme of building anticipation and excitement:

Recommended Toys:

1. **Teasing Toys:** Toys designed for teasing and slow build-up are perfect for this phase. These toys can help increase anticipation and heighten arousal over time.
   - **Example:** Feather ticklers, light paddles, or soft floggers can provide gentle stimulation and tease your partner, building up desire and excitement.
2. **Edging Vibrators:** Vibrators that allow for precise control of intensity are ideal for edging, a practice where you bring yourself or your partner close to orgasm and then back off to build anticipation.
   - **Example:** A multi-speed wand vibrator or a powerful bullet vibrator with adjustable settings can help you control the intensity and prolong the pleasure.
3. **Remote-Controlled Toys:** Remote-controlled toys add an element of surprise and anticipation. They can be controlled by your partner, creating a dynamic of suspense and excitement.
   - **Example:** A remote-controlled egg vibrator or a wearable panty vibrator can provide thrilling sensations and keep you on edge throughout the day or evening.
4. **Sensory Deprivation Toys:** Blindfolds and sensory deprivation toys can enhance anticipation by heightening other senses and creating an element of surprise.

- **Example:** A satin blindfold paired with noise-canceling headphones can immerse you in the sensations and build anticipation through the unknown.

5. **Couples' Toys:** Toys designed for couples can enhance intimacy and anticipation by allowing you to explore new sensations together.
   - **Example:** A couples' vibrator that can be worn during intercourse, providing simultaneous stimulation, can build excitement and deepen your connection.
6. **Bondage Gear:** Light bondage gear can add an element of control and suspense, increasing anticipation and heightening arousal.
   - **Example:** Soft cuffs or a silky rope can be used to gently restrain your partner, creating a sense of anticipation and excitement as you take control.

Recommended Practices:

1. **Edging and Teasing:** Practice edging by bringing yourself or your partner close to orgasm and then backing off to build anticipation. This technique can lead to more intense and satisfying climaxes.
   - **Practice:** Engage in a teasing session where you use a vibrator or your hands to stimulate your partner, bringing them close to orgasm multiple times before finally allowing them to climax.
2. **Extended Foreplay:** Focus on prolonged foreplay to build anticipation and enhance arousal. Use touch, kisses, and whispered words to create a sense of excitement and desire.
   - **Practice:** Spend an evening dedicated to foreplay, exploring each other's bodies and teasing each other with light touches, kisses, and caresses without rushing to intercourse.

3. **Surprise and Spontaneity:** Incorporate elements of surprise and spontaneity into your sexual routine. Plan unexpected intimate moments that catch your partner off guard and build anticipation.

    ◦ **Practice:** Surprise your partner with a spontaneous make-out session or a surprise date night that leads to a sensual encounter, keeping them guessing and excited.

4. **Sensory Play:** Engage in sensory play by using different textures, temperatures, and sensations to tease and arouse your partner. This can heighten anticipation and create a more immersive experience.

    ◦ **Practice:** Use a combination of feather ticklers, ice cubes, and warm oils to stimulate your partner's senses and build anticipation through varied sensations.

5. **Mindful Masturbation:** Practice mindful masturbation by focusing on the sensations and your body's responses without rushing to orgasm. This can increase sexual awareness and build anticipation.

    ◦ **Practice:** Set aside time for a solo session where you explore your body slowly and mindfully, paying attention to the buildup of pleasure and delaying climax.

6. **Fantasy Exploration:** Share and explore fantasies with your partner. Discussing and acting out fantasies can build anticipation and deepen your connection.

    ◦ **Practice:** Have a fantasy-sharing session where you and your partner take turns describing your fantasies in detail. Choose one to explore together, building anticipation and excitement.

Conclusion

The Waxing Crescent, with its themes of growth and building anticipation, offers a powerful opportunity to invigorate your sexual energy and explore new dimensions of pleasure. By understanding its influence, choosing the right toys, and adopting practices that align with this lunar phase, you can create deeply satisfying and transformative sexual experiences. Embrace the Waxing Crescent's energy to build anticipation, try new things, and deepen your connection with yourself and your partner. The following chapters will continue to explore the cosmic influences on sexuality, helping everyone discover the unique pleasures that align with their astrological profile.

Chapter 17: First Quarter - Taking Action
Influence of the First Quarter on Sexual Energy

The First Quarter Moon, occurring a week after the New Moon, marks a time of action, decision-making, and progress. This phase is characterized by a half-illuminated moon, symbolizing a balance between light and dark. Astrologically, the First Quarter is a period of overcoming challenges and taking decisive steps toward achieving goals. This energy significantly impacts our emotions, behaviors, and sexual dynamics.

Key Influences of the First Quarter on Sexual Energy:

1. **Decisive Action:** The First Quarter Moon encourages taking bold and decisive actions. In terms of sexuality, it's a time to actively pursue desires, make confident choices, and overcome any hesitations or barriers.

2. **Building Momentum:** This phase is about building momentum and moving forward. It's an ideal period for initiating new sexual activities, experimenting with new toys, and exploring different aspects of your sexuality.

3. **Overcoming Challenges:** The First Quarter Moon's energy supports overcoming obstacles and pushing through any resistance. This can be a time to address and resolve sexual issues or challenges in your relationship.

4. **Increased Confidence:** The assertive energy of this phase boosts confidence and encourages a proactive approach to sex. It's a time to express your desires openly and take the lead in intimate encounters.

5. **Balancing Energies:** With the moon half-illuminated, this phase represents a balance between light and dark. It's a time to find

harmony between different aspects of your sexual self and integrate them into a cohesive whole.

Recommended Toys and Practices for Initiative

Harnessing the energy of the First Quarter can lead to dynamic and empowering sexual experiences. Here are some recommended toys and practices that align with the theme of taking action and building momentum:

Recommended Toys:

1. **High-Powered Vibrators:** High-powered vibrators that offer intense and deep stimulation are perfect for this phase. These toys can help you take decisive action and explore new levels of pleasure.
   - **Example:** A powerful wand vibrator or a high-intensity bullet vibrator can provide strong and consistent stimulation, helping you take control of your pleasure.
2. **Dual-Stimulation Toys:** Toys that offer both internal and external stimulation simultaneously can help you explore multiple sensations at once, building momentum and excitement.
   - **Example:** A rabbit vibrator or a dual-action clitoral and G-spot vibrator can provide comprehensive pleasure, helping you achieve intense and satisfying orgasms.
3. **Remote-Controlled and App-Enabled Toys:** Remote-controlled toys add an element of playfulness and spontaneity. They allow you or your partner to take control, encouraging a proactive approach to pleasure.
   - **Example:** A remote-controlled vibrating egg or a wearable panty vibrator can provide unexpected thrills and help you take the initiative in your sexual experiences.
4. **Bondage and BDSM Gear:** Light bondage gear can enhance the sense of control and action, allowing you to explore power dynamics and take decisive steps in your sexual exploration.

- ◦ **Example:** Soft cuffs, a blindfold, or a beginner's bondage kit can help you and your partner explore new dynamics and take action in a safe and consensual manner.

5. **Penis Rings:** For those with penises, penis rings can enhance erection strength and duration, providing a boost of confidence and control in intimate encounters.
   - ◦ **Example:** A vibrating penis ring can add stimulation for both partners, helping you take decisive action and enhance mutual pleasure.

Recommended Practices:

1. **Initiating Intimacy:** Use the First Quarter's energy to take the initiative in your sexual relationship. Plan a special date night or surprise your partner with a spontaneous intimate moment.
   - ◦ **Practice:** Arrange a romantic evening with candles, soft music, and a sensual massage. Take the lead in guiding your partner through a series of pleasurable activities.
2. **Exploring New Techniques:** This phase is perfect for trying new sexual techniques and positions. Be bold and experiment with different ways to enhance pleasure and intimacy.
   - ◦ **Practice:** Research and try out new sexual positions or techniques that you haven't explored before. Take the lead in guiding your partner through these new experiences.
3. **Addressing Sexual Challenges:** The assertive energy of the First Quarter can help you address and resolve any sexual challenges or issues in your relationship. Have open and honest conversations about your needs and desires.
   - ◦ **Practice:** Schedule a time to discuss any sexual challenges or desires with your partner. Use this conversation to set goals and take action toward achieving them.
4. **Building Sexual Confidence:** Use this phase to boost your sexual confidence by exploring your body and desires. Masturbation

and self-exploration can help you gain a deeper understanding of what pleases you.

- ◦ **Practice:** Dedicate time to self-pleasure, experimenting with different toys and techniques. Focus on building your confidence and understanding your body's responses.

5. **Balancing Energies:** The First Quarter is a time to find balance between different aspects of your sexual self. Integrate your desires, fantasies, and realities into a harmonious whole.

- ◦ **Practice:** Reflect on your sexual experiences and desires. Identify areas where you may need to find balance, such as integrating fantasies with real-life experiences or balancing giving and receiving pleasure.

6. **Active Foreplay:** Engage in active and dynamic foreplay that builds anticipation and excitement. Use touch, kisses, and playful teasing to create a sense of momentum.

- ◦ **Practice:** Plan an extended foreplay session where you take turns teasing and pleasuring each other. Use toys, oral sex, and manual stimulation to build anticipation and excitement.

Conclusion

The First Quarter, with its themes of action and momentum, offers a powerful opportunity to invigorate your sexual energy and take decisive steps toward achieving your desires. By understanding its influence, choosing the right toys, and adopting practices that align with this lunar phase, you can create dynamic and empowering sexual experiences. Embrace the First Quarter's energy to take action, explore new techniques, and deepen your connection with yourself and your partner. The following chapters will continue to explore the cosmic influences on sexuality, helping everyone discover the unique pleasures that align with their astrological profile.

Chapter 18: Waxing Gibbous - Refinement and Focus
Influence of the Waxing Gibbous on Sexual Energy

The Waxing Gibbous Moon, occurring between the First Quarter and the Full Moon, symbolizes a time of refinement, focus, and preparation. This phase is characterized by a nearly full moon, indicating that the culmination of the lunar cycle is near. Astrologically, the Waxing Gibbous is a period of heightened anticipation and meticulous attention to detail. This energy influences our emotions, behaviors, and sexual dynamics by encouraging us to fine-tune our desires and prepare for ultimate fulfillment.

Key Influences of the Waxing Gibbous on Sexual Energy:

1. **Refinement and Perfection:** The Waxing Gibbous phase is about refining and perfecting. In terms of sexuality, it's a time to focus on enhancing techniques, exploring deeper levels of pleasure, and improving intimacy with your partner.

2. **Building Anticipation:** As the moon grows fuller, so does the sense of anticipation. This phase is perfect for engaging in activities that build sexual tension and heighten excitement, leading to a more satisfying climax.

3. **Focused Energy:** The energy of the Waxing Gibbous is concentrated and focused. It's an ideal period for concentrating on specific aspects of your sexual relationship that you want to improve or explore more deeply.

4. **Preparation for Fulfillment:** This phase is about preparing for the fullness of the Full Moon. It's a time to set the stage for a peak sexual experience by ensuring all elements are perfectly aligned.

5. **Attention to Detail:** The meticulous nature of the Waxing Gibbous encourages attention to detail. This can enhance the quality of your sexual experiences by focusing on the small nuances that make a significant difference.

Recommended Toys and Practices for Refinement

Harnessing the energy of the Waxing Gibbous can lead to exquisitely refined and deeply satisfying sexual experiences. Here are some recommended toys and practices that align with the theme of refinement and focus:

Recommended Toys:

1. **Precision Vibrators:** Precision vibrators designed for targeted stimulation are perfect for this phase. These toys allow for controlled and focused pleasure, helping you refine your techniques and explore specific erogenous zones.
   - **Example:** A pinpoint clitoral vibrator or a slim, curved G-spot vibrator can provide precise stimulation, allowing you to focus on areas that bring the most pleasure.
2. **Luxury Sex Toys:** High-quality sex toys made from premium materials offer a refined and luxurious experience. These toys often feature advanced settings and superior craftsmanship, enhancing the overall quality of your intimate moments.
   - **Example:** A luxury silicone vibrator with customizable vibration patterns or a hand-crafted glass dildo can elevate your sexual experience.
3. **Adjustable Couples' Toys:** Couples' toys that can be adjusted to fit different preferences and positions can help you and your partner refine your techniques and enhance mutual pleasure.
   - **Example:** An adjustable vibrating cock ring or a flexible couples' vibrator that can be worn in various ways can add versatility and refinement to your play.

4. **Sensual Massagers:** Full-body massagers that offer soothing vibrations can enhance relaxation and arousal. These toys help you focus on the sensory experience, refining your approach to touch and sensation.
   - **Example:** A high-end wand massager with multiple attachments can provide a range of sensations, helping you fine-tune your pleasure.

5. **Anal Training Kits:** For those exploring anal play, an anal training kit with different sizes and textures can help you gradually refine your techniques and build comfort and confidence.
   - **Example:** A set of graduated anal plugs or beads can provide a step-by-step approach to refining your anal play experience.

Recommended Practices:

1. **Focused Foreplay:** Use the Waxing Gibbous energy to engage in focused and intentional foreplay. Pay attention to your partner's responses and refine your techniques to enhance their pleasure.
   - **Practice:** Dedicate a session to exploring each other's bodies with touch, kisses, and gentle caresses. Use feedback to adjust your techniques and find what brings the most pleasure.

2. **Edging and Teasing:** Build anticipation by practicing edging and teasing. This technique involves bringing yourself or your partner close to orgasm and then backing off to build sexual tension and excitement.
   - **Practice:** Use a vibrator or your hands to stimulate your partner, bringing them to the brink of orgasm multiple times before allowing them to climax.

3. **Intimate Communication:** Engage in open and honest communication with your partner about your desires, boundaries, and

fantasies. Use this phase to refine your understanding of each other's needs.

- **Practice:** Have a "pleasure mapping" session where you discuss and explore each other's erogenous zones and preferred techniques. Use this information to enhance your intimate moments.

4. **Sensory Play:** Incorporate sensory play to heighten arousal and refine your sensory awareness. Use different textures, temperatures, and sensations to create a more immersive experience.

- **Practice:** Experiment with feather ticklers, ice cubes, warm oils, and scented candles to stimulate the senses and build anticipation.

5. **Mindful Masturbation:** Practice mindful masturbation by focusing on the sensations and your body's responses without rushing to orgasm. This can increase sexual awareness and help you refine your techniques.

- **Practice:** Set aside time for a solo session where you explore your body slowly and mindfully, paying attention to the buildup of pleasure and delaying climax.

6. **Romantic Rituals:** Create romantic rituals that enhance intimacy and connection. These rituals can set the stage for a more refined and meaningful sexual experience.

- **Practice:** Plan a romantic evening with a shared bath, a massage, and a candlelit dinner. Use this time to connect emotionally and physically, building anticipation for a more intimate encounter.

Conclusion

The Waxing Gibbous, with its themes of refinement and focus, offers a powerful opportunity to enhance your sexual energy and fine-tune your intimate experiences. By understanding its influence, choosing the right toys, and adopting practices that align with this lunar phase, you can create deeply satisfying and exquisitely refined sexual experiences.

Embrace the Waxing Gibbous's energy to refine your techniques, build anticipation, and deepen your connection with yourself and your partner. The following chapters will continue to explore the cosmic influences on sexuality, helping everyone discover the unique pleasures that align with their astrological profile.

Chapter 19: Full Moon - Peak Passion
Influence of the Full Moon on Sexual Energy

The Full Moon, a phase where the moon is fully illuminated and at its brightest, symbolizes culmination, peak energy, and heightened emotions. Astrologically, the Full Moon is a time of intensity, illumination, and the realization of desires. This energy profoundly influences our emotions, behaviors, and sexual dynamics by magnifying our feelings and passions, making it an ideal time for deep, passionate connections.

Key Influences of the Full Moon on Sexual Energy:

1. **Heightened Emotions:** The Full Moon amplifies emotions, making feelings more intense and raw. In terms of sexuality, this heightened emotional state can lead to deeper, more passionate encounters.

2. **Increased Libido:** The peak energy of the Full Moon often results in a surge in sexual desire and energy. It's a time when people feel more sexually charged and eager to express their passions.

3. **Intense Connections:** The illuminating power of the Full Moon enhances emotional and physical connections. This phase is perfect for exploring deeper levels of intimacy and bonding with your partner.

4. **Culmination of Desires:** The Full Moon represents the culmination of intentions set during the New Moon. It's a time to realize and fulfill sexual desires and fantasies that have been building up.

5. **Release and Liberation:** This phase encourages the release of inhibitions and the embracing of true desires. It's a time to let go of fears and fully immerse in the experience of pleasure.

Recommended Toys and Practices for Passion

Harnessing the energy of the Full Moon can lead to incredibly passionate and deeply fulfilling sexual experiences. Here are some recommended toys and practices that align with the theme of peak passion:

Recommended Toys:

1. **Powerful Wand Massagers:** Wand massagers are known for their intense and rumbly vibrations, making them perfect for the heightened energy of the Full Moon. These toys can deliver deep and satisfying pleasure, helping you fully express your passion.
   - **Example:** A powerful wand vibrator with multiple intensity settings can provide strong external stimulation, enhancing your experience of peak passion.
2. **Dual-Stimulation Vibrators:** Toys that offer both internal and external stimulation simultaneously are ideal for this phase. They can help you achieve intense and multifaceted pleasure.
   - **Example:** A rabbit vibrator or a dual-action clitoral and G-spot vibrator can provide comprehensive pleasure, helping you achieve powerful orgasms.
3. **Remote-Controlled and App-Enabled Toys:** Remote-controlled toys add an element of excitement and spontaneity. They allow you or your partner to take control, encouraging a playful and passionate approach to pleasure.
   - **Example:** A remote-controlled egg vibrator or a wearable panty vibrator can provide unexpected thrills and help you fully embrace the energy of the Full Moon.
4. **Bondage and BDSM Gear:** Light bondage gear can enhance the sense of control and intensity, allowing you to explore power dynamics and fully immerse in passionate play.

- **Example:** Soft cuffs, a blindfold, or a beginner's bondage kit can help you and your partner explore new dynamics and deepen your connection.

5. **Anal Toys:** For those exploring anal play, anal toys can provide intense and satisfying stimulation. This can be an exciting way to embrace the passionate energy of the Full Moon.

- **Example:** A vibrating anal plug or a set of graduated anal beads can add a new dimension to your play, enhancing the overall experience.

Recommended Practices:

1. **Intense Foreplay:** Use the Full Moon's energy to engage in intense and passionate foreplay. Focus on building anticipation and deepening your connection with your partner.

- **Practice:** Dedicate a session to exploring each other's bodies with touch, kisses, and gentle caresses. Use feedback to adjust your techniques and find what brings the most pleasure.

2. **Role-Playing and Fantasy:** This phase is perfect for exploring fantasies and role-playing scenarios. Embrace the heightened energy and let go of inhibitions to fully immerse in your desires.

- **Practice:** Plan a role-playing session where you and your partner act out a shared fantasy. Use costumes, props, and dialogue to enhance the experience and make it more immersive.

3. **Exploring Deep Connections:** The Full Moon's energy enhances emotional and physical connections. Use this time to deepen your bond with your partner through eye contact, touch, and intimate conversations.

- **Practice:** Engage in a practice of gazing into each other's eyes, holding hands, and sharing your deepest desires and fantasies. This can create a powerful sense of intimacy and connection.

4. **Embracing Passion:** Fully embrace the passionate energy of the Full Moon by letting go of inhibitions and expressing your desires openly. Use this time to explore new heights of pleasure and satisfaction.

   ◦ **Practice:** Plan an evening where you focus on fully expressing your passion. Use toys, techniques, and positions that you've always wanted to try but haven't had the chance to.

5. **Mindful Masturbation:** Practice mindful masturbation by focusing on the sensations and your body's responses without rushing to orgasm. This can increase sexual awareness and help you fully embrace the energy of the Full Moon.

   ◦ **Practice:** Set aside time for a solo session where you explore your body slowly and mindfully, paying attention to the buildup of pleasure and delaying climax.

6. **Sensory Play:** Incorporate sensory play to heighten arousal and enhance the overall experience. Use different textures, temperatures, and sensations to create a more immersive experience.

   ◦ **Practice:** Experiment with feather ticklers, ice cubes, warm oils, and scented candles to stimulate the senses and build anticipation.

Conclusion

The Full Moon, with its themes of peak energy and passion, offers a powerful opportunity to fully embrace your sexual energy and explore new heights of pleasure. By understanding its influence, choosing the right toys, and adopting practices that align with this lunar phase, you can create deeply passionate and fulfilling sexual experiences. Embrace the Full Moon's energy to express your desires, deepen your connection, and immerse yourself in the experience of peak passion. The following chapters will continue to explore the cosmic influences on sexuality, helping everyone discover the unique pleasures that align with their astrological profile.

Chapter 20: Waning Gibbous - Gratitude and Sharing
Influence of the Waning Gibbous on Sexual Energy

The Waning Gibbous Moon, occurring just after the Full Moon, symbolizes a time of reflection, gratitude, and sharing. This phase represents the diminishing of lunar illumination as the moon begins to wane, marking the transition from peak energy to a period of introspection and communal sharing. Astrologically, the Waning Gibbous is a time to appreciate the abundance that the Full Moon brought, share experiences, and nurture relationships. This energy influences our emotions, behaviors, and sexual dynamics by encouraging a sense of gratitude, emotional connection, and mutual enjoyment.

Key Influences of the Waning Gibbous on Sexual Energy:

1. **Reflection and Gratitude:** The Waning Gibbous is a time to reflect on recent experiences and express gratitude for the pleasures and connections enjoyed during the Full Moon. This can deepen emotional bonds and enhance the sense of intimacy.

2. **Nurturing Relationships:** This phase encourages nurturing and caring for your partner. It's a time to focus on mutual satisfaction, emotional connection, and the sharing of intimate moments.

3. **Communal Sharing:** The energy of the Waning Gibbous supports sharing and communal experiences. It's an ideal period for exploring mutual pleasures and creating shared sexual experiences that foster closeness.

4. **Emotional Connection:** The reflective nature of this phase enhances emotional sensitivity and connection. It's a time to engage in activities that strengthen your emotional bond and create a sense of togetherness.

5. **Savoring Pleasure:** The Waning Gibbous encourages savoring and appreciating the pleasures experienced. This can enhance the

quality of your sexual encounters by focusing on the joy and satisfaction of shared experiences.

Recommended Toys and Practices for Sharing

Harnessing the energy of the Waning Gibbous can lead to deeply nurturing and mutually satisfying sexual experiences. Here are some recommended toys and practices that align with the theme of gratitude and sharing:

Recommended Toys:

1. **Couples' Vibrators:** Couples' vibrators are designed to be used during intercourse, providing simultaneous stimulation for both partners. These toys enhance mutual pleasure and help create a shared experience of intimacy.
    - **Example:** A couples' vibrator that can be worn during sex, offering clitoral and internal stimulation for one partner while providing additional sensations for the other.
2. **Remote-Controlled Toys:** Remote-controlled toys add an element of playfulness and shared control. They allow partners to take turns controlling the toy, enhancing the sense of mutual engagement and enjoyment.
    - **Example:** A remote-controlled vibrating egg or a wearable panty vibrator can provide thrilling sensations and allow for playful interaction between partners.
3. **Massage Wands:** Full-body massagers that offer soothing vibrations can be used for mutual massages. These toys help create a relaxing and intimate atmosphere, enhancing emotional connection.
    - **Example:** A high-end wand massager with multiple attachments can provide a range of sensations, allowing partners to explore and share pleasure.

4. **Erotic Games and Kits:** Erotic games and kits designed for couples can enhance intimacy and provide fun ways to explore each other's desires and fantasies.
   - **Example:** An erotic board game that includes challenges, questions, and activities focused on building intimacy and enhancing sexual connection.
5. **Sensual Accessories:** Accessories such as blindfolds, feather ticklers, and massage oils can enhance the sensory experience and create a shared journey of exploration and pleasure.
   - **Example:** A kit that includes a blindfold, feather tickler, and scented massage oil can enhance the sensory experience and build anticipation and intimacy.

Recommended Practices:

1. **Mutual Massages:** Use the Waning Gibbous energy to engage in mutual massages. This practice can enhance relaxation, build anticipation, and deepen the emotional connection between partners.
   - **Practice:** Take turns giving each other full-body massages using warm, aromatic oils. Focus on creating a relaxing and intimate atmosphere, and use the time to connect emotionally and physically.
2. **Expressing Gratitude:** Share expressions of gratitude with your partner for the pleasures and connections enjoyed. This practice can deepen your bond and enhance the sense of mutual appreciation.
   - **Practice:** Spend time after your intimate encounter sharing what you appreciate about each other and the experience. Use this time to express gratitude and reinforce your emotional connection.
3. **Engaging in Intimate Conversations:** The reflective nature of this phase encourages deep and meaningful conversations. Use

this time to share your desires, fantasies, and reflections on your sexual experiences.

- ○ **Practice:** Have a "pillow talk" session where you and your partner discuss your recent sexual experiences, what you enjoyed, and what you'd like to explore in the future.

4. **Exploring Mutual Fantasies:** The Waning Gibbous is a perfect time to explore shared fantasies and desires. Engage in activities that align with your mutual interests and enhance your connection.

- ○ **Practice:** Share and explore a mutual fantasy with your partner. Use role-playing, costumes, or props to bring the fantasy to life and create a shared experience of pleasure.

5. **Practicing Sensory Play:** Incorporate sensory play to heighten arousal and create a shared journey of exploration. Use different textures, temperatures, and sensations to enhance the overall experience.

- ○ **Practice:** Experiment with feather ticklers, ice cubes, warm oils, and scented candles to stimulate the senses and build anticipation and intimacy.

6. **Savoring Slow Lovemaking:** Focus on slow and sensual lovemaking that emphasizes emotional connection and mutual satisfaction. Take the time to savor each moment and fully enjoy the experience.

- ○ **Practice:** Plan an extended lovemaking session where you take your time exploring each other's bodies, using slow and deliberate movements to build anticipation and deepen the connection.

Conclusion

The Waning Gibbous, with its themes of gratitude and sharing, offers a powerful opportunity to deepen your sexual energy and enhance your emotional connection. By understanding its influence, choosing the right toys, and adopting practices that align with this lunar phase, you can create deeply nurturing and mutually satisfying sexual experiences. Embrace the Waning Gibbous's energy to express gratitude, share intimate moments, and nurture your relationship. The following chapters will continue to explore the cosmic influences on sexuality, helping everyone discover the unique pleasures that align with their astrological profile.

Chapter 21: Last Quarter - Reflection and Release
Influence of the Last Quarter on Sexual Energy

The Last Quarter Moon, occurring a week after the Full Moon, symbolizes a time of reflection, release, and letting go. This phase is characterized by the moon being half-illuminated and half in shadow, indicating a balance between holding on and letting go. Astrologically, the Last Quarter is a period of introspection, evaluation, and preparation for new beginnings. This energy influences our emotions, behaviors, and sexual dynamics by encouraging us to reflect on past experiences, release what no longer serves us, and prepare for renewal.

Key Influences of the Last Quarter on Sexual Energy:

1. **Reflection and Evaluation:** The Last Quarter is a time to reflect on recent experiences and evaluate what has been learned. In terms of sexuality, it's a time to assess your desires, behaviors, and relationships, and identify areas for growth and improvement.

2. **Releasing and Letting Go:** This phase encourages releasing negative emotions, limiting beliefs, and unfulfilling patterns. It's an ideal period for letting go of sexual inhibitions, past disappointments, and anything that hinders your sexual fulfillment.

3. **Introspection and Clarity:** The Last Quarter's energy supports introspection and gaining clarity. It's a time to connect with your inner self, understand your true desires, and set intentions for the future.

4. **Balancing and Harmonizing:** The balance between light and dark during this phase symbolizes finding harmony between different aspects of your sexual self. It's a time to integrate your experiences and find a balanced approach to your sexuality.

5. **Preparation for Renewal:** The Last Quarter prepares you for the new cycle ahead. It's a time to cleanse and purify your energy, making space for new experiences and opportunities.

Recommended Toys and Practices for Reflection

Harnessing the energy of the Last Quarter can lead to deeply introspective and transformative sexual experiences. Here are some recommended toys and practices that align with the theme of reflection and release:

Recommended Toys:

1. **Mindful Masturbation Toys:** Toys that promote slow, deliberate stimulation are ideal for this phase. These toys can help you connect with your body and explore your desires with mindfulness and intention.
    ◦ **Example:** A slow-speed vibrator or a gently curved G-spot vibrator can provide precise and controlled stimulation, encouraging mindful exploration.
2. **Sensual Massagers:** Full-body massagers that offer soothing vibrations can enhance relaxation and introspection. These toys help create a calming and reflective atmosphere, perfect for letting go of stress and tension.
    ◦ **Example:** A high-end wand massager with multiple settings can provide a range of soothing sensations, helping you relax and reflect.
3. **Kegel Exercisers:** For those looking to enhance their sexual health and awareness, Kegel exercisers can help strengthen pelvic floor muscles and increase sensitivity.
    ◦ **Example:** A set of weighted Kegel balls or a smart Kegel exerciser that connects to an app for guided exercises can support pelvic health and sexual awareness.
4. **Temperature Play Toys:** Toys designed for temperature play can enhance sensory exploration and deepen your connection

with your body. These toys can provide a unique and reflective experience.

- **Example:** Glass or metal dildos that can be heated or cooled offer versatile and exciting sensations, encouraging a deeper connection with your physical self.

5. **Erotic Journaling Kits:** Kits that combine erotic toys with journaling prompts can help you reflect on your sexual experiences and desires, promoting personal growth and self-awareness.

- **Example:** A journaling kit that includes a small vibrator, scented candles, and guided prompts for erotic reflection can create a holistic and introspective experience.

Recommended Practices:

1. **Erotic Journaling:** Use the Last Quarter's energy to engage in erotic journaling. Reflect on your sexual experiences, desires, and fantasies, and write about what you've learned and what you'd like to explore in the future.

- **Practice:** Set aside time to write in a journal about your recent sexual experiences. Reflect on what brought you pleasure, what you learned about yourself, and any areas you'd like to improve or explore further.

2. **Mindful Masturbation:** Practice mindful masturbation by focusing on the sensations and your body's responses without rushing to orgasm. This can increase sexual awareness and help you connect with your inner self.

- **Practice:** Dedicate a session to mindful masturbation, using slow and deliberate movements to explore your body. Pay attention to the buildup of pleasure and the sensations you experience.

3. **Meditative Practices:** Incorporate meditation into your sexual routine to enhance introspection and relaxation. Use guided

meditations or breathing exercises to center yourself and prepare for a reflective sexual experience.

- ○ **Practice:** Begin your intimate session with a guided meditation or deep breathing exercise. Focus on clearing your mind and connecting with your body, setting the stage for a reflective and mindful experience.

4. **Couples' Reflection:** Share a reflective practice with your partner by discussing your recent sexual experiences, what you've enjoyed, and what you'd like to improve. This can enhance your connection and mutual understanding.

- ○ **Practice:** Have a "reflection night" where you and your partner talk about your recent sexual experiences. Share what you appreciated, what you learned, and any desires or fantasies you'd like to explore together.

5. **Sensory Exploration:** Engage in sensory exploration to heighten your awareness and deepen your connection with your body. Use different textures, temperatures, and sensations to create a unique and introspective experience.

- ○ **Practice:** Experiment with sensory play by using feather ticklers, ice cubes, warm oils, and scented candles. Focus on the sensations and how they make you feel, reflecting on your responses.

6. **Letting Go Rituals:** Create rituals that symbolize letting go of past inhibitions, disappointments, or negative experiences. This can help you release what no longer serves you and make space for new beginnings.

- ○ **Practice:** Write down any negative thoughts or experiences you'd like to release on a piece of paper. Perform a ritual where you safely burn the paper, symbolizing the release of these burdens and the embrace of new opportunities.

Conclusion

The Last Quarter, with its themes of reflection and release, offers a powerful opportunity to deepen your sexual energy and prepare for new beginnings. By understanding its influence, choosing the right toys, and adopting practices that align with this lunar phase, you can create deeply introspective and transformative sexual experiences. Embrace the Last Quarter's energy to reflect on your desires, release what no longer serves you, and prepare for renewal. The following chapters will continue to explore the cosmic influences on sexuality, helping everyone discover the unique pleasures that align with their astrological profile.

Chapter 22: Waning Crescent - Rest and Preparation
Influence of the Waning Crescent on Sexual Energy

The Waning Crescent Moon, occurring just before the New Moon, symbolizes a time of rest, renewal, and preparation. This phase represents the final stage of the lunar cycle, where the moon's illumination gradually decreases until it is no longer visible. Astrologically, the Waning Crescent is a period of introspection, healing, and quiet reflection. This energy influences our emotions, behaviors, and sexual dynamics by encouraging us to slow down, rest, and prepare for the new cycle ahead.

Key Influences of the Waning Crescent on Sexual Energy:

1. **Rest and Renewal:** The Waning Crescent is a time to rest and recharge. In terms of sexuality, it's a period for gentle, nurturing experiences that promote relaxation and healing.

2. **Introspection and Healing:** This phase encourages introspection and emotional healing. It's an ideal time to reflect on past experiences, address any unresolved emotions, and nurture your emotional well-being.

3. **Quiet Reflection:** The reflective nature of the Waning Crescent supports quiet, intimate moments. It's a time to connect with your partner on a deeper, more emotional level, fostering a sense of closeness and understanding.

4. **Preparation for New Beginnings:** This phase prepares you for the new cycle ahead. It's a time to cleanse and purify your energy, making space for new experiences and opportunities in your sexual life.

5. **Gentle Connection:** The Waning Crescent encourages gentle, nurturing connections. It's a time to focus on soft, tender touches and slow, deliberate movements that enhance intimacy and relaxation.

Recommended Toys and Practices for Rest

Harnessing the energy of the Waning Crescent can lead to deeply relaxing and restorative sexual experiences. Here are some recommended toys and practices that align with the theme of rest and preparation:

Recommended Toys:

1. **Soothing Vibrators:** Vibrators designed for gentle, soothing stimulation are perfect for this phase. These toys can help you relax and unwind, providing soft and comforting sensations.
   - **Example:** A low-intensity vibrator or a silicone wand massager with a gentle setting can provide soothing vibrations, enhancing relaxation and comfort.
2. **Sensual Massagers:** Full-body massagers that offer calming vibrations can enhance relaxation and introspection. These toys help create a tranquil and nurturing atmosphere, perfect for winding down.
   - **Example:** A high-end wand massager with multiple settings can provide a range of gentle sensations, helping you relax and reflect.
3. **Heated Toys:** Toys that offer gentle heat can enhance relaxation and provide a comforting, warming sensation. These toys are ideal for promoting a sense of calm and well-being.
   - **Example:** A heated massage wand or a warming vibrator can provide soothing warmth, enhancing the overall experience of relaxation.
4. **Soft Bondage Gear:** For those who enjoy light bondage, soft, non-restrictive gear can add a sense of security and comfort without being too intense.
   - **Example:** A silk or velvet blindfold and soft cuffs can create a gentle and nurturing experience, enhancing the sense of closeness and trust.

5. **Bath and Shower Toys:** Waterproof toys that can be used in the bath or shower can enhance relaxation and provide a soothing, sensory experience.
   - **Example:** A waterproof bullet vibrator or a silicone dildo can be used in the bath or shower, providing a relaxing and comforting experience.

Recommended Practices:

1. **Gentle Foreplay:** Use the Waning Crescent's energy to engage in gentle and nurturing foreplay. Focus on soft touches, slow caresses, and tender kisses that promote relaxation and intimacy.
   - **Practice:** Dedicate a session to gentle foreplay, using soft touches and slow movements to explore each other's bodies. Focus on creating a calming and intimate atmosphere.
2. **Mindful Breathing:** Incorporate mindful breathing exercises into your intimate moments. Deep, slow breaths can enhance relaxation and help you connect with your body and your partner.
   - **Practice:** Begin your intimate session with a few minutes of deep breathing. Inhale slowly and deeply, hold for a moment, and then exhale slowly. Focus on your breath and the sensations in your body.
3. **Couples' Massage:** Share a relaxing massage with your partner. Use warm, aromatic oils and soothing strokes to create a sense of calm and connection.
   - **Practice:** Take turns giving each other a full-body massage. Use long, slow strokes and gentle pressure to relax and soothe each other's muscles, enhancing the sense of intimacy and relaxation.
4. **Bath or Shower Together:** Enjoy a relaxing bath or shower with your partner. The warm water and soothing sensations can enhance relaxation and create a calming, intimate atmosphere.

- **Practice:** Run a warm bath with essential oils or bath salts. Get into the bath together and take turns washing each other, using gentle, slow movements to enhance relaxation and connection.

5. **Reflective Journaling:** Use this phase to reflect on your sexual experiences and desires through journaling. Writing about your thoughts and feelings can promote self-awareness and emotional healing.

   - **Practice:** Set aside time to write in a journal about your recent sexual experiences, what you've learned, and what you'd like to explore in the future. Reflect on your emotions and any areas for growth or healing.

6. **Quiet Time Together:** Spend quiet, intimate time with your partner without the pressure of sexual activity. Cuddle, talk, and enjoy each other's company, focusing on emotional connection and relaxation.

   - **Practice:** Plan an evening where you simply spend time together in a quiet, comfortable setting. Cuddle, talk about your day, and enjoy each other's presence without the expectation of sex.

Conclusion

The Waning Crescent, with its themes of rest and preparation, offers a powerful opportunity to deepen your sexual energy and nurture your emotional well-being. By understanding its influence, choosing the right toys, and adopting practices that align with this lunar phase, you can create deeply relaxing and restorative sexual experiences. Embrace the Waning Crescent's energy to rest, reflect, and prepare for new beginnings in your sexual life. The following chapters will continue to explore the cosmic influences on sexuality, helping everyone discover the unique pleasures that align with their astrological profile.

Chapter 23: Cosmic Events and Their Influence on Sexuality Explanation of Various Cosmic Events and Their Astrological Significance

Astrology is deeply intertwined with the movements of celestial bodies and cosmic events, which significantly influence our lives, emotions, and sexual energy. Understanding the astrological significance of these events can enhance our awareness and help us harness their energies to enrich our sexual experiences.

Eclipses

Lunar Eclipses: Occur when the Earth passes between the Sun and the Moon, casting a shadow on the Moon. Lunar eclipses are associated with emotional release, transformation, and powerful shifts in consciousness. They bring hidden emotions to the surface and encourage us to let go of what no longer serves us.

Solar Eclipses: Happen when the Moon passes between the Earth and the Sun, blocking the Sun's light. Solar eclipses symbolize new beginnings, significant changes, and the initiation of new cycles. They are a time of renewal and the manifestation of new intentions.

Retrogrades

Mercury Retrograde: Occurs when Mercury appears to move backward in its orbit. This period is associated with communication breakdowns, misunderstandings, and delays. It is a time for introspection, reviewing past experiences, and resolving unfinished business.

Venus Retrograde: Happens when Venus appears to move backward. This period is linked to reevaluations of love, relationships, and self-worth. It's a time to reflect on romantic connections, assess personal values, and heal past emotional wounds.

Mars Retrograde: Occurs when Mars appears to move backward. This period is associated with a reassessment of desires, motivation, and actions. It's a time to reflect on personal goals, address unresolved conflicts, and realign with true passions.

Meteor Showers

Meteor showers are celestial events where multiple meteors are observed radiating from one point in the sky. They symbolize moments of sudden inspiration, heightened creativity, and bursts of energy. These events encourage spontaneity and embracing new experiences.

Recommended Toys and Practices for Each Cosmic Event

Harnessing the energies of these cosmic events can lead to profound and transformative sexual experiences. Here are some recommended toys and practices for each event:

Lunar Eclipses

Recommended Toys:

1. **Transformative Vibrators:** Vibrators that offer powerful and deep stimulation are ideal for this phase. They can help release pent-up emotions and facilitate transformative experiences.
   - **Example:** A wand massager with multiple intensity settings can provide deep, satisfying vibrations, helping you release and transform emotional energy.
2. **Shadow Work Journaling Kits:** Kits that combine erotic toys with journaling prompts for shadow work can help you explore hidden desires and release emotional blocks.
   - **Example:** A kit that includes a small vibrator, scented candles, and guided prompts for exploring and releasing hidden desires.

Recommended Practices:

1. **Emotional Release Rituals:** Use the energy of the lunar eclipse to engage in rituals that promote emotional release and transformation.
   - **Practice:** Perform a cleansing ritual where you write down emotions or experiences you wish to release. Safely burn the paper while focusing on letting go and transforming.

2. **Shadow Exploration:** Reflect on hidden desires and fantasies, bringing them into the light for exploration and acceptance.
   - **Practice:** Set aside time for erotic journaling, where you explore and write about your hidden desires and fantasies. Use this reflection to embrace and transform your sexual energy.

Solar Eclipses
Recommended Toys:

1. **New Beginnings Kits:** Kits designed to facilitate new experiences and explore new aspects of sexuality are perfect for solar eclipses.
   - **Example:** A couples' kit that includes various toys, such as a vibrating cock ring, a bullet vibrator, and a blindfold, to explore new dynamics and sensations.
2. **Initiation Vibrators:** Vibrators that offer a range of functions and settings to explore new sensations and techniques.
   - **Example:** A versatile rabbit vibrator with customizable vibration patterns and intensity settings can help you explore new forms of pleasure.

Recommended Practices:

1. **Intention Setting:** Use the solar eclipse to set new sexual intentions and explore new aspects of your sexuality.
   - **Practice:** Perform an intention-setting ritual where you write down your sexual goals and desires. Meditate on these intentions while using a favorite toy to anchor the new energy.
2. **Exploring New Techniques:** Try new sexual techniques and positions that align with your intentions and desires.

- **Practice:** Experiment with different sexual positions and techniques that you've always wanted to try. Use this time to explore and initiate new experiences.

Mercury Retrograde
Recommended Toys:

1. **Communication Enhancers:** Toys that facilitate mutual pleasure and enhance communication are ideal for this phase.
    - **Example:** A remote-controlled vibrator that you and your partner can use to explore long-distance control and communication.
2. **Reflective Vibrators:** Vibrators designed for slow, deliberate stimulation that encourage introspection and mindfulness.
    - **Example:** A low-intensity vibrator with gentle settings can provide soothing vibrations, helping you relax and reflect.

Recommended Practices:

1. **Mindful Communication:** Use Mercury Retrograde to focus on improving communication and resolving misunderstandings.
    - **Practice:** Engage in a practice where you and your partner share your desires and needs openly. Use a remote-controlled toy to explore and enhance communication during intimate moments.
2. **Reflective Masturbation:** Practice mindful masturbation to connect with your inner self and reflect on your desires.
    - **Practice:** Dedicate time to mindful masturbation, using slow and deliberate movements to explore your body and reflect on your sexual needs and experiences.

Venus Retrograde
Recommended Toys:

1. **Self-Love Toys:** Toys that promote self-love and enhance personal pleasure are perfect for this phase.
   - **Example:** A luxurious clitoral vibrator that offers gentle, nurturing stimulation can enhance self-love and appreciation.
2. **Healing Kits:** Kits that combine erotic toys with tools for emotional healing and self-care.
   - **Example:** A self-love kit that includes a vibrator, massage oil, and guided self-care prompts can support emotional healing and self-discovery.

Recommended Practices:

1. **Self-Love Rituals:** Use Venus Retrograde to engage in self-love rituals that promote emotional healing and self-worth.
   - **Practice:** Perform a self-love ritual where you pamper yourself with a warm bath, a gentle massage, and the use of a favorite toy. Focus on appreciating and nurturing your body.
2. **Reevaluating Relationships:** Reflect on your romantic relationships and assess areas for improvement and healing.
   - **Practice:** Have a heart-to-heart conversation with your partner about your relationship. Use this time to discuss your needs, boundaries, and desires, and explore ways to deepen your connection.

Mars Retrograde
Recommended Toys:

1. **Passion Igniters:** Toys that enhance passion and intensity are ideal for this phase.

- ◦ **Example:** A powerful vibrating cock ring or a dual-stimulation vibrator can increase intensity and passion during intimate moments.

2. **Conflict Resolution Kits:** Kits that combine erotic toys with tools for resolving conflicts and enhancing passion.
   - ◦ **Example:** A couples' kit that includes a vibrating cock ring, a bullet vibrator, and communication prompts can help address conflicts and reignite passion.

Recommended Practices:

1. **Reigniting Passion:** Use Mars Retrograde to reignite passion and address any unresolved conflicts in your relationship.
   - ◦ **Practice:** Plan a passionate date night where you focus on reconnecting and reigniting your sexual energy. Use toys and techniques that enhance intensity and passion.
2. **Reflecting on Desires:** Reflect on your desires and motivations, and realign with your true passions.
   - ◦ **Practice:** Engage in a reflective practice where you write down your sexual desires and goals. Use this time to reconnect with what truly excites and motivates you.

Meteor Showers
Recommended Toys:

1. **Spontaneous Pleasure Toys:** Toys designed for spontaneous and playful exploration are perfect for meteor showers.
   - ◦ **Example:** A remote-controlled vibrator or a portable bullet vibrator can provide unexpected thrills and spontaneous pleasure.
2. **Creative Exploration Kits:** Kits that combine erotic toys with tools for creative exploration and inspiration.

- ◦ **Example:** A creativity kit that includes a vibrator, sensory play items, and guided prompts for exploring new fantasies and desires.

Recommended Practices:

1. **Embracing Spontaneity:** Use the energy of meteor showers to embrace spontaneity and try new things.
   - ◦ **Practice:** Plan a spontaneous sexual adventure with your partner. Use portable toys and explore new locations or activities that excite and inspire you.
2. **Creative Fantasy Exploration:** Use the heightened creativity of meteor showers to explore new fantasies and desires.
   - ◦ **Practice:** Set aside time to share and explore fantasies with your partner. Use role-playing, costumes, or props to bring your fantasies to life and create a shared experience of excitement and pleasure.

Conclusion

Cosmic events, with their unique energies and influences, offer powerful opportunities to enhance your sexual energy and explore new dimensions of pleasure. By understanding the astrological significance of these events, choosing the right toys, and adopting practices that align with their energies, you can create profound and transformative sexual experiences. Embrace the cosmic energies to deepen your connection with yourself and your partner, and discover the unique pleasures that align with your astrological profile. The following chapters will continue to explore the cosmic influences on sexuality, helping everyone unlock the full potential of their cosmic pleasures.

Chapter 24: Planet Alignments and Sexual Compatibility
Explanation of Major Planet Alignments and Their Impact on Relationships and Sexuality

Planetary alignments occur when planets form specific geometric patterns with each other in the sky. These alignments can significantly influence our emotions, behaviors, and relationships, including our sexual dynamics. Understanding the impact of these alignments can help us navigate our relationships more effectively and enhance our sexual compatibility.

Key Planet Alignments and Their Astrological Significance:

1. **Conjunctions:** Occur when two planets are very close together in the sky, often in the same zodiac sign. Conjunctions amplify the energies of the involved planets, creating intense and focused energy. In relationships, this alignment can enhance intimacy, passion, and a sense of unity.

2. **Oppositions:** Happen when two planets are directly opposite each other in the sky, creating a push-pull dynamic. Oppositions can bring tension and conflict but also provide opportunities for growth and balance. In relationships, this alignment can challenge partners to find harmony and mutual understanding.

3. **Trines:** Occur when two planets form a 120-degree angle, creating a harmonious and supportive connection. Trines enhance

flow, ease, and cooperation. In relationships, this alignment can promote harmony, understanding, and shared pleasure.

4. **Squares:** Happen when two planets form a 90-degree angle, creating tension and friction. Squares can bring challenges and conflicts but also opportunities for growth and transformation. In relationships, this alignment can push partners to address issues and work towards resolution.

5. **Sextiles:** Occur when two planets form a 60-degree angle, creating opportunities and potential. Sextiles enhance communication, cooperation, and mutual support. In relationships, this alignment can promote exploration, collaboration, and mutual pleasure.

How to Use Sex Toys to Enhance Compatibility and Connection During These Alignments

Harnessing the energies of planetary alignments can lead to enhanced compatibility and deeper connection in your sexual relationships. Here are some recommended toys and practices for each alignment:

Conjunctions

Recommended Toys:

1. **Intensifying Vibrators:** Vibrators that offer powerful and deep stimulation are ideal for this phase. They can help amplify the intense energy of conjunctions, creating passionate and focused experiences.
   - **Example:** A wand massager with multiple intensity settings can provide deep, satisfying vibrations, helping you connect deeply with your partner.

2. **Couples' Kits:** Kits designed for mutual pleasure and exploration can enhance the sense of unity and intimacy.
   - **Example:** A couples' kit that includes a vibrating cock ring, a bullet vibrator, and a blindfold can enhance shared pleasure and create a sense of closeness.

Recommended Practices:

1. **Shared Intensity:** Use the energy of conjunctions to engage in intense and passionate sexual experiences. Focus on deep connection and mutual pleasure.
     - **Practice:** Plan an evening dedicated to intense lovemaking. Use toys and techniques that enhance intensity and passion, and focus on connecting deeply with your partner.
2. **Unity Rituals:** Engage in rituals that enhance the sense of unity and closeness in your relationship.
     - **Practice:** Perform a unity ritual where you meditate together, holding hands and focusing on your shared intentions and desires. Use a favorite toy to anchor the energy of unity and connection.

Oppositions
Recommended Toys:

1. **Balancing Toys:** Toys that offer a balance of internal and external stimulation can help navigate the push-pull dynamics of oppositions.
     - **Example:** A rabbit vibrator that provides both clitoral and G-spot stimulation can help balance and harmonize conflicting energies.
2. **Communication Enhancers:** Remote-controlled toys that facilitate mutual pleasure and enhance communication are ideal for this phase.
     - **Example:** A remote-controlled vibrating egg or a wearable panty vibrator can help explore long-distance control and communication, enhancing mutual understanding.

Recommended Practices:

1. **Balancing Acts:** Use the energy of oppositions to find balance and harmony in your sexual relationship. Focus on addressing any conflicts and finding mutual pleasure.
   - **Practice:** Engage in a balancing act where you take turns pleasuring each other, using toys that offer dual stimulation. Focus on creating a harmonious and balanced experience.
2. **Conflict Resolution:** Use this time to address and resolve any conflicts or misunderstandings in your relationship.
   - **Practice:** Have an open and honest conversation about your needs and desires. Use a remote-controlled toy to enhance communication and mutual understanding during intimate moments.

Trines
Recommended Toys:

1. **Harmonizing Vibrators:** Vibrators that offer smooth, consistent stimulation are perfect for trines. They can help enhance the harmonious energy of this alignment, creating a sense of flow and ease.
   - **Example:** A luxury silicone vibrator with customizable vibration patterns and intensity settings can provide smooth and harmonious pleasure.
2. **Sensory Play Kits:** Kits that include a variety of sensory play items can enhance the sense of harmony and cooperation.
   - **Example:** A sensory play kit that includes feather ticklers, blindfolds, and massage oils can enhance the overall sensory experience, promoting harmony and shared pleasure.

Recommended Practices:

1. **Flow and Ease:** Use the energy of trines to engage in smooth and harmonious sexual experiences. Focus on creating a sense of flow and mutual enjoyment.
    - **Practice:** Plan a sensual evening where you use toys and techniques that enhance smooth and consistent pleasure. Focus on creating a harmonious and flowing experience.
2. **Shared Sensory Exploration:** Engage in sensory play that enhances the overall sensory experience and promotes harmony.
    - **Practice:** Explore different textures, temperatures, and sensations together, using a sensory play kit. Focus on creating a harmonious and immersive experience.

Squares
Recommended Toys:

1. **Transformative Toys:** Toys that offer intense and transformative stimulation are ideal for squares. They can help navigate the challenges and friction of this alignment, creating opportunities for growth and transformation.
    - **Example:** A powerful dual-stimulation vibrator or a vibrating anal plug can provide intense and transformative pleasure, helping you address and resolve conflicts.
2. **Conflict Resolution Kits:** Kits that combine erotic toys with tools for resolving conflicts and enhancing passion.
    - **Example:** A couples' kit that includes a vibrating cock ring, a bullet vibrator, and communication prompts can help address conflicts and reignite passion.

Recommended Practices:

1. **Addressing Challenges:** Use the energy of squares to address and resolve any challenges or conflicts in your relationship. Focus on finding mutual pleasure and understanding.

- ◦ **Practice:** Plan a session where you address any conflicts or challenges in your relationship. Use toys that offer intense and transformative stimulation to enhance the experience.
2. **Transformative Rituals:** Engage in rituals that promote transformation and growth in your relationship.
    - ◦ **Practice:** Perform a transformative ritual where you meditate together, focusing on your shared intentions for growth and transformation. Use a favorite toy to anchor the energy of transformation and renewal.

Sextiles

Recommended Toys:

1. **Exploration Kits:** Kits designed to facilitate exploration and creativity are perfect for sextiles. They can help enhance the cooperative and communicative energy of this alignment.
    - ◦ **Example:** A creativity kit that includes a vibrator, sensory play items, and guided prompts for exploring new fantasies and desires.
2. **Communication Enhancers:** Remote-controlled toys that facilitate mutual pleasure and enhance communication are ideal for this phase.
    - ◦ **Example:** A remote-controlled vibrating egg or a wearable panty vibrator can help explore long-distance control and communication, enhancing mutual understanding.

Recommended Practices:

1. **Creative Exploration:** Use the energy of sextiles to engage in creative and exploratory sexual experiences. Focus on communicating openly and exploring new fantasies and desires.
    - ◦ **Practice:** Plan a creative exploration session where you use toys and techniques that enhance communication and

mutual pleasure. Focus on exploring new fantasies and desires together.

2. **Collaborative Play:** Engage in activities that promote cooperation and mutual support in your sexual relationship.
   - **Practice:** Use a communication-enhancing toy to explore long-distance control and mutual pleasure. Focus on creating a collaborative and supportive experience.

Conclusion

Planetary alignments, with their unique energies and influences, offer powerful opportunities to enhance your sexual compatibility and deepen your connection with your partner. By understanding the astrological significance of these alignments, choosing the right toys, and adopting practices that align with their energies, you can create profound and transformative sexual experiences. Embrace the cosmic energies to deepen your connection with yourself and your partner, and discover the unique pleasures that align with your astrological profile. The following chapters will continue to explore the cosmic influences on sexuality, helping everyone unlock the full potential of their cosmic pleasures.

Chapter 25: The Wiccan Wheel of the Year and Sexual Energy
Overview of the Wiccan Wheel of the Year and Its Eight Sabbats
The Wiccan Wheel of the Year is a cycle of eight Sabbats, or seasonal festivals, that celebrate the changing seasons and natural rhythms of the Earth. These Sabbats mark significant points in the solar year and are times of celebration, reflection, and connection with nature. Each Sabbat carries its own unique energy and significance, influencing our emotions, behaviors, and sexual dynamics.

The Eight Sabbats

1. **Samhain (October 31st - November 1st):** Samhain marks the end of the harvest and the beginning of winter. It is a time for honoring ancestors, reflecting on the past, and embracing transformation and renewal.
2. **Yule (December 20th - 23rd):** Yule celebrates the winter solstice, the longest night of the year, and the return of the light. It is a time for introspection, renewal, and celebrating the rebirth of the sun.
3. **Imbolc (February 1st - 2nd):** Imbolc marks the beginning of spring and the awakening of new life. It is a time for purification, renewal, and setting intentions for the future.
4. **Ostara (March 20th - 23rd):** Ostara celebrates the spring equinox, a time of balance between light and dark. It is a time for fertility, growth, and new beginnings.

5. **Beltane (April 30th - May 1st):** Beltane is a festival of fertility and passion, celebrating the height of spring. It is a time for exuberance, joy, and celebrating the union of the divine feminine and masculine.

6. **Litha (June 20th - 23rd):** Litha marks the summer solstice, the longest day of the year. It is a time for celebration, abundance, and joy, honoring the sun at its peak.

7. **Lammas (August 1st - 2nd):** Lammas celebrates the first harvest and the abundance of the Earth. It is a time for gratitude, sharing, and nurturing.

8. **Mabon (September 20th - 23rd):** Mabon marks the autumn equinox, a time of balance between light and dark. It is a time for reflection, balance, and giving thanks for the harvest.

Recommended Toys and Practices for Each Sabbat

Harnessing the energies of the Wiccan Sabbats can lead to profound and enriching sexual experiences. Here are some recommended toys and practices for each Sabbat:

Samhain

Recommended Toys:

1. **Transformative Vibrators:** Vibrators that offer powerful and deep stimulation can help harness the transformative energy of Samhain.
   - **Example:** A wand massager with multiple intensity settings can provide deep, satisfying vibrations, helping you connect with the transformative energy of this Sabbat.

2. **Shadow Work Journaling Kits:** Kits that combine erotic toys with journaling prompts for shadow work can help you explore hidden desires and release emotional blocks.
   - **Example:** A kit that includes a small vibrator, scented candles, and guided prompts for exploring and releasing hidden desires.

Recommended Practices:

1. **Emotional Release Rituals:** Use Samhain's energy to engage in rituals that promote emotional release and transformation.
    - **Practice:** Perform a cleansing ritual where you write down emotions or experiences you wish to release. Safely burn the paper while focusing on letting go and transforming.
2. **Shadow Exploration:** Reflect on hidden desires and fantasies, bringing them into the light for exploration and acceptance.
    - **Practice:** Set aside time for erotic journaling, where you explore and write about your hidden desires and fantasies. Use this reflection to embrace and transform your sexual energy.

Yule
Recommended Toys:

1. **Soothing Vibrators:** Vibrators designed for gentle, soothing stimulation are perfect for the introspective and renewing energy of Yule.
    - **Example:** A low-intensity vibrator or a silicone wand massager with a gentle setting can provide soothing vibrations, enhancing relaxation and comfort.
2. **Heated Toys:** Toys that offer gentle heat can enhance relaxation and provide a comforting, warming sensation.
    - **Example:** A heated massage wand or a warming vibrator can provide soothing warmth, enhancing the overall experience of relaxation.

Recommended Practices:

1. **Renewal Rituals:** Use Yule's energy to engage in rituals that promote renewal and rebirth.

- **Practice:** Perform a renewal ritual where you meditate on your intentions for the coming year. Use a favorite toy to anchor the energy of renewal and new beginnings.
2. **Introspective Masturbation:** Practice mindful masturbation to connect with your inner self and reflect on your desires.
    - **Practice:** Dedicate time to mindful masturbation, using slow and deliberate movements to explore your body and reflect on your sexual needs and experiences.

Imbolc
Recommended Toys:

1. **Purifying Toys:** Toys that promote cleansing and renewal are ideal for Imbolc.
    - **Example:** A luxury clitoral vibrator that offers gentle, nurturing stimulation can enhance self-love and appreciation.
2. **Healing Kits:** Kits that combine erotic toys with tools for emotional healing and self-care.
    - **Example:** A self-love kit that includes a vibrator, massage oil, and guided self-care prompts can support emotional healing and self-discovery.

Recommended Practices:

1. **Purification Rituals:** Use Imbolc's energy to engage in rituals that promote purification and renewal.
    - **Practice:** Perform a purification ritual where you cleanse your body with a warm bath, using essential oils and bath salts. Focus on releasing negative energy and embracing renewal.
2. **Setting Intentions:** Reflect on your sexual desires and set intentions for the coming cycle.

- ○ **Practice:** Write down your sexual goals and desires, meditating on them while using a favorite toy to anchor the new energy.

Ostara
Recommended Toys:

1. **Fertility and Growth Toys:** Toys that promote fertility and growth are perfect for Ostara.
   - ○ **Example:** A dual-stimulation vibrator that provides both clitoral and G-spot stimulation can enhance fertility and growth.
2. **Sensual Massagers:** Full-body massagers that offer soothing vibrations can enhance relaxation and introspection.
   - ○ **Example:** A high-end wand massager with multiple settings can provide a range of soothing sensations, helping you relax and reflect.

Recommended Practices:

1. **Fertility Rituals:** Use Ostara's energy to engage in rituals that promote fertility and growth.
   - ○ **Practice:** Perform a fertility ritual where you meditate on your intentions for growth and new beginnings. Use a favorite toy to anchor the energy of fertility and abundance.
2. **Sensual Exploration:** Engage in sensory play that enhances the overall sensory experience and promotes growth.
   - ○ **Practice:** Explore different textures, temperatures, and sensations together, using a sensory play kit. Focus on creating a harmonious and immersive experience.

Beltane
Recommended Toys:

1. **Passion Igniters:** Toys that enhance passion and intensity are ideal for Beltane.
    - **Example:** A powerful vibrating cock ring or a dual-stimulation vibrator can increase intensity and passion during intimate moments.
2. **Creative Exploration Kits:** Kits that combine erotic toys with tools for creative exploration and inspiration.
    - **Example:** A creativity kit that includes a vibrator, sensory play items, and guided prompts for exploring new fantasies and desires.

Recommended Practices:

1. **Celebrating Union:** Use Beltane's energy to celebrate the union of the divine feminine and masculine. Engage in activities that promote passion and connection.
    - **Practice:** Plan a passionate date night where you focus on reconnecting and celebrating your union. Use toys and techniques that enhance intensity and passion.
2. **Exploring Fantasies:** Use the heightened creativity of Beltane to explore new fantasies and desires.
    - **Practice:** Set aside time to share and explore fantasies with your partner. Use role-playing, costumes, or props to bring your fantasies to life and create a shared experience of excitement and pleasure.

Litha
Recommended Toys:

1. **Joyful Vibrators:** Vibrators that offer playful and joyful stimulation are perfect for Litha.

- **Example:** A remote-controlled vibrator or a portable bullet vibrator can provide unexpected thrills and spontaneous pleasure.

2. **Exploration Kits:** Kits designed to facilitate exploration and creativity are perfect for Litha.
   - **Example:** A creativity kit that includes a vibrator, sensory play items, and guided prompts for exploring new fantasies and desires.

Recommended Practices:

1. **Celebrating Abundance:** Use Litha's energy to celebrate abundance and joy. Engage in activities that promote playfulness and connection.
   - **Practice:** Plan a joyful date night where you focus on celebrating your connection and abundance. Use toys and techniques that enhance playfulness and pleasure.
2. **Embracing Spontaneity:** Use the energy of Litha to embrace spontaneity and try new things.
   - **Practice:** Plan a spontaneous sexual adventure with your partner. Use portable toys and explore new locations or activities that excite and inspire you.

Lammas
Recommended Toys:

1. **Gratitude Toys:** Toys that promote gratitude and nurturing are ideal for Lammas.
   - **Example:** A luxurious clitoral vibrator that offers gentle, nurturing stimulation can enhance self-love and appreciation.
2. **Sensual Massagers:** Full-body massagers that offer soothing vibrations can enhance relaxation and introspection.

- **Example:** A high-end wand massager with multiple settings can provide a range of soothing sensations, helping you relax and reflect.

Recommended Practices:

1. **Gratitude Rituals:** Use Lammas's energy to engage in rituals that promote gratitude and nurturing.
   - **Practice:** Perform a gratitude ritual where you and your partner take turns expressing what you appreciate about each other. Use a favorite toy to enhance the feeling of closeness and mutual appreciation.
2. **Nurturing Experiences:** Focus on nurturing and caring for your partner. Engage in activities that promote relaxation and emotional connection.
   - **Practice:** Plan an evening where you give each other full-body massages with warm, aromatic oils. Use gentle strokes and soothing touches to create a nurturing and intimate atmosphere.

Mabon
Recommended Toys:

1. **Balancing Vibrators:** Vibrators that offer a balance of internal and external stimulation can help harness the balancing energy of Mabon.
   - **Example:** A rabbit vibrator that provides both clitoral and G-spot stimulation can help balance and harmonize energies.
2. **Sensory Play Kits:** Kits that include a variety of sensory play items can enhance the sense of balance and harmony.

- ◦ **Example:** A sensory play kit that includes feather ticklers, blindfolds, and massage oils can enhance the overall sensory experience, promoting balance and shared pleasure.

Recommended Practices:

1. **Balance Rituals:** Use Mabon's energy to engage in rituals that promote balance and harmony.
   - ◦ **Practice:** Perform a balance ritual where you meditate together, focusing on finding balance in your relationship. Use a favorite toy to anchor the energy of balance and harmony.
2. **Shared Sensory Exploration:** Engage in sensory play that enhances the overall sensory experience and promotes balance.
   - ◦ **Practice:** Explore different textures, temperatures, and sensations together, using a sensory play kit. Focus on creating a harmonious and immersive experience.

Conclusion

The Wiccan Wheel of the Year, with its unique energies and influences, offers powerful opportunities to deepen your sexual energy and enhance your emotional connection with your partner. By understanding the significance of each Sabbat, choosing the right toys, and adopting practices that align with their energies, you can create profound and enriching sexual experiences. Embrace the seasonal energies to deepen your connection with yourself and your partner, and discover the unique pleasures that align with your astrological profile. The following chapters will continue to explore the cosmic influences on sexuality, helping everyone unlock the full potential of their cosmic pleasures.

Chapter 26: Integrating It All

Tips for Combining Astrological Insights, Cosmic Events, Moon Phases, Planetary Alignments, and the Wiccan Wheel of the Year in Your Sexual Practices

Integrating astrological insights, cosmic events, moon phases, planetary alignments, and the Wiccan Wheel of the Year can create a holistic and deeply enriching approach to your sexual practices. By understanding the unique energies and influences of these elements, you can enhance your sexual experiences and deepen your connection with yourself and your partner.

1. Understanding Your Astrological Profile

Begin by understanding your astrological profile, including your Sun, Moon, and Rising signs, as well as the positions of Venus and Mars. These elements provide a foundation for understanding your core personality, emotional needs, and sexual inclinations. Use this knowledge to tailor your sexual practices to your unique astrological influences.

- **Tip:** Create a birth chart and study the positions of key planets. Reflect on how these placements influence your sexual energy and preferences.

2. Aligning with Moon Phases

The moon phases provide a cyclical rhythm that can enhance different aspects of your sexual energy. By aligning your sexual practices with the moon phases, you can create a balanced and harmonious sexual experience.

- **Tip:** Use the New Moon for setting sexual intentions, the Waxing Crescent for building anticipation, the Full Moon for peak passion, and the Waning Crescent for rest and preparation.

3. Harnessing Planetary Alignments

Planetary alignments can significantly impact your sexual energy and relationships. Understanding the effects of conjunctions, oppositions, trines, squares, and sextiles can help you navigate these influences and enhance your sexual compatibility.

- **Tip:** Pay attention to upcoming planetary alignments and plan your sexual activities accordingly. Use conjunctions for deep connection, oppositions for balancing acts, trines for harmonious flow, squares for addressing challenges, and sextiles for creative exploration.

4. Embracing Cosmic Events

Cosmic events such as eclipses, retrogrades, and meteor showers offer unique opportunities to deepen your sexual experiences. Each event carries its own energy and significance, influencing your sexual dynamics in different ways.

- **Tip:** Use lunar eclipses for emotional release, solar eclipses for new beginnings, Mercury retrograde for mindful communication, Venus retrograde for self-love, Mars retrograde for reigniting passion, and meteor showers for spontaneous exploration.

5. Celebrating the Wiccan Wheel of the Year

The Wiccan Wheel of the Year offers a seasonal rhythm that can enhance your sexual energy and connection with nature. Each Sabbat provides a unique energy that can be integrated into your sexual practices.

- **Tip:** Celebrate Samhain with shadow exploration, Yule with renewal rituals, Imbolc with purification, Ostara with fertility rituals, Beltane with passionate celebrations, Litha with joyful exploration, Lammas with gratitude rituals, and Mabon with balance rituals.

How to Create a Personalized Sex Toy Astrology Calendar

Creating a personalized sex toy astrology calendar can help you integrate these various elements into your sexual practices, providing a structured and intentional approach to your sexual exploration.

Step 1: Identify Key Dates

Begin by identifying key dates that are significant in astrology, cosmic events, moon phases, planetary alignments, and the Wiccan Wheel of the Year. Mark these dates on your calendar to keep track of upcoming influences.

- **Tip:** Use online resources or astrology apps to track moon phases, planetary alignments, and cosmic events.

Step 2: Plan Your Practices

For each key date, plan specific sexual practices that align with the energy of the event. Consider incorporating recommended toys and rituals that enhance the specific influences of the date.

- **Tip:** For a New Moon, plan an intention-setting ritual with a favorite toy. For a Full Moon, engage in intense and passionate lovemaking with powerful vibrators. For a Wiccan Sabbat, celebrate with themed rituals and toys.

Step 3: Incorporate Astrological Insights

Integrate your personal astrological insights into your calendar. Reflect on how the positions of your Sun, Moon, Venus, and Mars influence your sexual energy and preferences, and plan practices that align with these influences.

- **Tip:** If your Venus is in a passionate sign like Scorpio, plan intense and transformative sexual experiences during significant Venus alignments.

Step 4: Reflect and Adjust

Regularly reflect on your experiences and adjust your calendar as needed. Pay attention to how different influences impact your sexual energy and satisfaction, and make changes to enhance your overall experience.

- **Tip:** Keep a journal to track your sexual experiences, noting the influences of different astrological elements and cosmic events. Use this reflection to refine your practices and calendar.

Encouragement to Explore and Experiment with Different Combinations

Exploring and experimenting with different combinations of astrological insights, cosmic events, moon phases, planetary alignments, and the Wiccan Wheel of the Year can lead to profound and transformative sexual experiences. Embrace the journey of discovery and allow yourself the freedom to try new things and adjust your practices based on your experiences.

- **Tip:** Stay open to new experiences and trust your intuition. Allow yourself to be guided by the energies of the cosmos and your inner desires.
- **Tip:** Share your journey with your partner and encourage them to explore and experiment with you. This can deepen your connection and enhance your mutual pleasure.

Conclusion

Integrating astrological insights, cosmic events, moon phases, planetary alignments, and the Wiccan Wheel of the Year into your sexual practices can create a holistic and deeply enriching approach to your sexuality. By understanding the unique energies and influences of these elements, you can enhance your sexual experiences and deepen your connection with yourself and your partner. Embrace the cosmic journey, create a personalized sex toy astrology calendar, and explore the full potential of your cosmic pleasures.

Conclusion

Summary of Key Points

In *Cosmic Pleasures: Sex Toy Astrology for Every Sign*, we have explored the fascinating intersection of astrology, cosmic events, moon phases, planetary alignments, and the Wiccan Wheel of the Year, all through the lens of enhancing sexual pleasure and intimacy. Here's a recap of the key points covered in this comprehensive guide:

1. **Astrological Insights:**
   - Understanding your Sun, Moon, and Rising signs, along with the positions of Venus and Mars, is crucial in comprehending your core personality, emotional needs, and sexual inclinations.
   - Each zodiac sign has unique sexual characteristics, and recognizing these can help tailor your sexual practices to your astrological profile.

2. **Moon Phases:**
   - The lunar cycle influences our sexual energy, with each phase offering distinct opportunities for enhancing intimacy and pleasure.
   - Aligning your sexual practices with the New Moon, Waxing Crescent, First Quarter, Waxing Gibbous, Full Moon, Waning Gibbous, Last Quarter, and Waning Crescent phases can create a balanced and harmonious sexual experience.

3. **Planetary Alignments:**
   - Conjunctions, oppositions, trines, squares, and sextiles all have significant impacts on our relationships and sexual energy.
   - Understanding these alignments can help you navigate their influences, enhancing compatibility and deepening connections.

4. **Cosmic Events:**
   - Eclipses, retrogrades, and meteor showers offer unique energies that can profoundly affect our sexual dynamics.
   - Utilizing the specific influences of these events can lead to transformative and enriching sexual experiences.

5. **Wiccan Wheel of the Year:**
   - The eight Sabbats (Samhain, Yule, Imbolc, Ostara, Beltane, Litha, Lammas, Mabon) mark significant seasonal transitions and offer distinct energies for enhancing sexual practices.
   - Celebrating these Sabbats with themed rituals and toys can deepen your connection with nature and your partner.

6. **Creating a Personalized Sex Toy Astrology Calendar:**
   - Integrating astrological insights, cosmic events, moon phases, planetary alignments, and the Wiccan Wheel of the Year into a personalized calendar can provide a structured and intentional approach to your sexual exploration.
   - Regular reflection and adjustment of your practices based on your experiences can refine and enhance your sexual journey.

Final Thoughts on Embracing Your Cosmic Sexuality

Embracing your cosmic sexuality is about recognizing and harnessing the powerful energies of the cosmos to enhance your intimate experiences. It's about understanding how the movements of celestial bodies and the rhythms of nature influence your emotions, behaviors, and sexual energy. By aligning your sexual practices with these cosmic influences, you can create a deeply fulfilling and harmonious sexual life.

Remember, your cosmic sexuality is unique to you. It's shaped by your astrological profile, your personal experiences, and your desires. Embrace this uniqueness and use the insights and practices outlined in this guide to explore and enhance your sexual journey.

Encouragement to Keep Exploring and Enjoying Your Sexual Journey

Your sexual journey is a lifelong adventure filled with opportunities for growth, discovery, and pleasure. The cosmic elements we've explored in this book provide a rich and dynamic framework for enhancing your intimate experiences, but they are just the beginning.

Keep exploring and experimenting with different combinations of astrological insights, cosmic events, moon phases, planetary alignments, and the Wiccan Wheel of the Year. Stay open to new experiences and trust your intuition. Allow yourself the freedom to try new things and adjust your practices based on your experiences.

Share your journey with your partner and encourage them to explore and experiment with you. This can deepen your connection, enhance your mutual pleasure, and create a stronger bond.

Above all, enjoy the journey. Embrace the joy, the passion, and the deep connection that come from aligning your sexual practices with the cosmos. Celebrate your sexuality, honor your desires, and let the cosmic energies guide you to new heights of pleasure and fulfillment.

Thank you for joining us on this cosmic journey. May your path be filled with love, pleasure, and profound connection.

Appendix A: Glossary of Terms

Types of Adult Toys

Anal Beads: A string of beads designed for anal insertion. The beads vary in size and are gradually inserted and removed to enhance pleasure.

Blindfold: A sensory deprivation tool used to block vision, heightening other senses and increasing anticipation and arousal.

Bullet Vibrator: A small, discreet vibrator typically used for clitoral stimulation. Compact and often powerful, it's great for pinpointed pleasure.

Butt Plug: A tapered plug designed for anal insertion, often used to enhance sexual pleasure and prepare for anal sex. Some models may vibrate or have decorative elements.

Chastity Device: A device worn over the genitals to prevent sexual activity. Often used in BDSM play to enforce control and denial.

Clitoral Pump: A device designed to increase blood flow to the clitoris, enhancing sensitivity and arousal.

Cock Ring: A ring worn around the base of the penis to enhance erection strength and duration, often equipped with a vibrating component for added stimulation.

Couples' Vibrator: A vibrator designed to be used by both partners during intercourse, providing simultaneous stimulation to enhance mutual pleasure.

Dildo: A phallic-shaped sex toy designed for penetration. Can be made from various materials such as silicone, glass, or metal.

Double-Ended Dildo: A dildo designed with two ends for dual penetration or to be used by two partners simultaneously.

Dual-Stimulation Vibrator: A vibrator that provides both internal and external stimulation simultaneously, commonly known as a rabbit vibrator.

Electro-Stimulation Toys: Toys that use mild electrical currents to provide unique sensations, often used in BDSM play for an added layer of intensity.

Feather Tickler: A toy used for light, teasing touches, enhancing sensory play and anticipation.

Fleshlight: A male masturbator designed to mimic the feel of vaginal, anal, or oral sex. Often shaped like a flashlight for discreet storage.

G-Spot Vibrator: A vibrator designed with a curved shape to target the G-spot in women, providing intense internal stimulation.

Glass Dildo: A dildo made of glass, known for its smooth texture and ability to be heated or cooled for temperature play.

Heated Toys: Toys that can be warmed up to provide a comforting, soothing sensation during use, enhancing relaxation and pleasure.

Kegel Exercisers: Devices used to strengthen the pelvic floor muscles. Often used by women to enhance sexual pleasure and pelvic health.

Massage Wand: A powerful, often corded, vibrator used for external stimulation. Known for its strong, rumbly vibrations.

Nipple Clamps: Clamps designed to be attached to the nipples, often used to enhance arousal and sensitivity through mild to moderate pressure.

Penis Pump: A device designed to create a vacuum around the penis, increasing blood flow and potentially enhancing erection strength and size.

Prostate Massager: A toy designed to stimulate the prostate gland in men, often used for enhancing orgasmic pleasure.

Remote-Controlled Vibrator: A vibrator that can be controlled remotely, either through a wireless remote or a smartphone app, allowing for interactive play.

Sensory Play Kits: Kits that include various items like feather ticklers, blindfolds, and massage oils to enhance the sensory experience during intimate play.

Silicone Vibrator: A vibrator made from body-safe silicone, known for its smooth texture and ease of cleaning.

Strap-On: A harness with an attached dildo, worn by one partner to penetrate the other. Often used in same-sex couples or for role reversal in heterosexual couples.

Suction Cup Dildo: A dildo with a suction cup base, allowing it to be attached to flat surfaces for hands-free play.

Vibrating Anal Plug: An anal plug equipped with a vibrating component for enhanced stimulation and pleasure during anal play.

Vibrating Cock Ring: A cock ring with a built-in vibrator to provide added stimulation for both partners during intercourse.

Warming Lube: Lubricant that provides a warming sensation, enhancing pleasure and sensitivity during use.

Astrological Terms and Events

Conjunction: An astrological aspect where two planets appear very close together in the sky, amplifying each other's energies.

Full Moon: The phase of the moon when it is fully illuminated. Associated with peak energy, heightened emotions, and culmination.

Lunar Eclipse: Occurs when the Earth passes between the Sun and the Moon, casting a shadow on the Moon. Associated with emotional release and transformation.

Mars Retrograde: A period when Mars appears to move backward in its orbit. Linked to reassessment of desires, motivation, and actions.

Mercury Retrograde: A period when Mercury appears to move backward in its orbit. Associated with communication breakdowns, misunderstandings, and delays.

Moon Phases: The cyclical changes of the moon, including New Moon, Waxing Crescent, First Quarter, Waxing Gibbous, Full Moon, Waning Gibbous, Last Quarter, and Waning Crescent.

New Moon: The phase of the moon when it is not visible from Earth. Associated with new beginnings, setting intentions, and introspection.

Opposition: An astrological aspect where two planets are directly opposite each other in the sky, creating a push-pull dynamic.

Planetary Alignments: The positions of planets in relation to each other, influencing various aspects of life, including relationships and sexuality.

Retrograde: A period when a planet appears to move backward in its orbit. Different planets' retrogrades have specific influences, such as Mercury (communication) and Venus (relationships).

Sextile: An astrological aspect where two planets form a 60-degree angle, creating opportunities and potential for growth.

Solar Eclipse: Occurs when the Moon passes between the Earth and the Sun, blocking the Sun's light. Symbolizes new beginnings and significant changes.

Square: An astrological aspect where two planets form a 90-degree angle, creating tension and opportunities for growth through challenges.

Trine: An astrological aspect where two planets form a 120-degree angle, creating a harmonious and supportive connection.

Waning Crescent: The final phase of the moon before the New Moon. Associated with rest, renewal, and preparation for new beginnings.

Waning Gibbous: The phase following the Full Moon, characterized by a decrease in illumination. Associated with gratitude, reflection, and sharing.

Waxing Crescent: The phase following the New Moon, characterized by increasing illumination. Associated with building anticipation and growth.

Waxing Gibbous: The phase leading up to the Full Moon, characterized by nearly full illumination. Associated with refinement, focus, and preparation for peak experiences.

Wiccan Wheel of the Year

Beltane (April 30th - May 1st): A festival of fertility and passion, celebrating the height of spring with exuberance and joy.

Imbolc (February 1st - 2nd): Marks the beginning of spring and the awakening of new life. A time for purification, renewal, and setting intentions.

Lammas (August 1st - 2nd): Celebrates the first harvest and the abundance of the Earth. A time for gratitude, sharing, and nurturing.

Litha (June 20th - 23rd): Marks the summer solstice, the longest day of the year. A time for celebration, abundance, and joy.

Mabon (September 20th - 23rd): Marks the autumn equinox, a time of balance between light and dark. A time for reflection, balance, and giving thanks for the harvest.

Ostara (March 20th - 23rd): Celebrates the spring equinox, a time of balance between light and dark. A time for fertility, growth, and new beginnings.

Samhain (October 31st - November 1st): Marks the end of the harvest and the beginning of winter. A time for honoring ancestors, reflecting on the past, and embracing transformation.

Yule (December 20th - 23rd): Celebrates the winter solstice, the longest night of the year, and the return of the light. A time for introspection, renewal, and celebrating the rebirth of the sun.

This glossary provides a comprehensive reference to help you navigate and integrate the rich tapestry of astrological insights, cosmic events, moon phases, planetary alignments, and the Wiccan Wheel of the Year into your sexual practices. Understanding these terms will enhance your journey through *Cosmic Pleasures: Sex Toy Astrology for Every Sign* and support you in unlocking the full potential of your cosmic sexuality.

Appendix B: Resources for Further Reading
Books on Astrology

1. **"The Only Astrology Book You'll Ever Need" by Joanna Martine Woolfolk**
   - A comprehensive guide to astrology, covering everything from birth charts to the influences of the planets and the zodiac signs.
2. **"Astrology for the Soul" by Jan Spiller**
   - An insightful exploration of how your North Node can reveal your life's purpose and help you understand your soul's mission.
3. **"The Inner Sky: How to Make Wiser Choices for a More Fulfilling Life" by Steven Forrest**
   - A practical and engaging introduction to astrological principles, focusing on how to use astrology for personal growth.
4. **"Astrology for Real Relationships: Understanding You, Me, and How We All Get Along" by Jessica Lanyadoo and T. Greenaway**
   - A modern take on astrology, offering advice on how to navigate relationships using astrological insights.
5. **"Parker's Astrology: The Definitive Guide to Using Astrology in Every Aspect of Your Life" by Julia and Derek Parker**
   - A detailed and visually appealing guide to astrology, perfect for both beginners and advanced students.

Books on Sexuality and Sexual Practices

1. **"The Guide to Getting It On!" by Paul Joannides**

- A comprehensive and entertaining guide to sex, covering everything from anatomy to techniques and emotional aspects.

2. **"Come As You Are: The Surprising New Science that Will Transform Your Sex Life" by Emily Nagoski**
   - An exploration of the science of sex, focusing on how understanding your body can lead to a more fulfilling sex life.

3. **"She Comes First: The Thinking Man's Guide to Pleasuring a Woman" by Ian Kerner**
   - A practical guide for men on how to pleasure their female partners, emphasizing the importance of female orgasm.

4. **"The New Topping Book" and "The New Bottoming Book" by Dossie Easton and Janet W. Hardy**
   - Two essential books for anyone interested in BDSM, covering the roles of top and bottom, and offering advice on safe and consensual play.

5. **"Urban Tantra: Sacred Sex for the Twenty-First Century" by Barbara Carrellas**
   - A modern take on tantra, offering techniques and practices for integrating spirituality and sexuality.

Books on the Wiccan Wheel of the Year and Pagan Practices

1. **"The Wicca Year: Spells, Rituals, Holiday Celebrations, and Reflections for Every Season" by Judy Ann Nock**
   - A practical guide to celebrating the Wiccan Sabbats, with rituals, spells, and reflections for each season.

2. **"The Complete Book of Witchcraft" by Raymond Buckland**
   - A comprehensive guide to Wiccan practices, including rituals for the Sabbats and Esbats, tools, and the philosophy of Wicca.

3. **"Wicca: A Guide for the Solitary Practitioner" by Scott Cunningham**

- A classic book on Wicca, focusing on how to practice as a solitary witch and celebrate the Wheel of the Year.

4. **"The Green Witch: Your Complete Guide to the Natural Magic of Herbs, Flowers, Essential Oils, and More" by Arin Murphy-Hiscock**
   - A detailed guide to green witchcraft, emphasizing the connection with nature and the cycles of the seasons.

5. **"Sabbats: A Witch's Approach to Living the Old Ways" by Edain McCoy**
   - An exploration of the eight Sabbats, with rituals, recipes, and crafts to celebrate the Wheel of the Year.

Websites and Online Resources

1. **Astro.com**
   - A comprehensive astrology website offering free birth charts, detailed astrological reports, and educational articles on various aspects of astrology.

2. **Cafe Astrology**
   - A user-friendly site providing free astrology reports, daily horoscopes, and in-depth articles on astrological topics.

3. **The Astrology Podcast**
   - A podcast featuring discussions on astrology, interviews with experts, and insights into astrological phenomena.

4. **BDSM Wiki**
   - An extensive resource for BDSM terminology, practices, and safety tips, useful for both beginners and experienced practitioners.

5. **Scarleteen**
   - A sex education website offering comprehensive information on sexuality, relationships, and sexual health for young adults.

6. **Autostraddle's Queer Sex Education Series**

- A collection of articles focusing on queer sex education, offering advice and insights on various aspects of queer sexuality.

YouTube Channels and Podcasts

1. **"Astrology with Heather" (YouTube)**
   - Heather provides detailed monthly forecasts, birth chart readings, and educational videos on various astrological topics.
2. **"The Astrology Podcast"**
   - Hosted by Chris Brennan, this podcast features in-depth discussions on astrology, interviews with astrologers, and insights into current astrological events.
3. **"Sex With Dr. Jess" (Podcast)**
   - Hosted by sexologist Dr. Jess O'Reilly, this podcast covers a wide range of topics related to sexuality, relationships, and sexual health.
4. **"The Lightworkers Lounge" (Podcast)**
   - A podcast that blends astrology, spirituality, and personal growth, offering insights and discussions on various esoteric topics.
5. **"Savage Lovecast" (Podcast)**
   - Hosted by Dan Savage, this podcast offers advice on sex, relationships, and kink, featuring guest experts and listener questions.

Online Communities and Forums

1. **Astrology Weekly Forum**
   - An active community where members discuss astrological charts, interpretations, and share insights and experiences.
2. **r/astrology (Reddit)**

- A subreddit dedicated to astrology, where users share information, ask questions, and discuss various astrological topics.

3. **r/sex (Reddit)**
   - A subreddit where users can ask questions, share experiences, and discuss all aspects of sex and sexuality.

4. **The Pagan Forum**
   - A community for pagans and Wiccans to discuss their beliefs, practices, and celebrate the Wheel of the Year together.

5. **FetLife**
   - A social networking site for the BDSM, fetish, and kink community, offering forums, groups, and events for like-minded individuals.

These resources provide a wealth of information for further exploring the intersections of astrology, sexuality, and cosmic influences. Whether you're looking to deepen your understanding of astrological principles, discover new sexual practices, or connect with like-minded individuals, these books, websites, podcasts, and communities will support and enhance your journey through *Cosmic Pleasures: Sex Toy Astrology for Every Sign*.

Appendix C: Suggested Retailers for Sex Toys

Finding high-quality and safe sex toys is essential for a fulfilling and satisfying experience. Below is a list of recommended retailers known for their wide selection, quality products, and excellent customer service. These retailers cater to various preferences and needs, ensuring that you can find the perfect toy to enhance your sexual journey.

Online Retailers

1. Lovehoney

- **Website:** www.lovehoney.com
- **Description:** Lovehoney is a well-known retailer offering a wide range of sex toys, lingerie, and sexual wellness products. They are praised for their discreet packaging, excellent customer service, and extensive product reviews.

2. Babeland

- **Website:** www.babeland.com
- **Description:** Babeland is dedicated to promoting sexual wellness and pleasure. They offer a curated selection of high-quality sex toys, educational resources, and workshops. Their focus on inclusivity and body-safe products makes them a trusted retailer.

3. SheVibe

- **Website:** www.shevibe.com
- **Description:** SheVibe is known for its unique and creative approach to sex toy retail, featuring a comic book-style website.

They offer a vast array of sex toys, accessories, and educational materials, emphasizing body-safe and high-quality products.

4. Good Vibrations

- **Website:** www.goodvibes.com
- **Description:** Good Vibrations is a pioneering retailer in the sex toy industry, offering a diverse selection of products for all genders and orientations. They focus on education, sexual health, and customer satisfaction.

5. The Pleasure Chest

- **Website:** www.thepleasurechest.com
- **Description:** The Pleasure Chest is a well-established retailer with a commitment to sexual education and inclusivity. They offer a wide range of toys, lingerie, and accessories, along with informative workshops and events.

6. Smitten Kitten

- **Website:** www.smittenkittenonline.com
- **Description:** Smitten Kitten specializes in body-safe sex toys and promotes sexual health and education. They provide a carefully curated selection of high-quality products and prioritize customer education.

7. Peepshow Toys

- **Website:** www.peepshowtoys.com
- **Description:** Peepshow Toys is dedicated to offering non-toxic, body-safe sex toys. They have a wide range of products for various

preferences and needs, and they emphasize customer education and safety.

Specialty Retailers
8. Tantus

- **Website:** www.tantusinc.com
- **Description:** Tantus specializes in high-quality silicone sex toys that are body-safe and durable. They offer a wide range of dildos, vibrators, and other accessories known for their superior craftsmanship.

9. Lelo

- **Website:** www.lelo.com
- **Description:** Lelo is a luxury sex toy brand known for its elegant design and high-tech features. They offer a range of premium vibrators, massagers, and couples' toys that combine aesthetics with functionality.

10. We-Vibe

- **Website:** www.we-vibe.com
- **Description:** We-Vibe is renowned for its innovative couples' toys and remote-controlled vibrators. Their products are designed to enhance intimacy and provide versatile pleasure options.

11. Fun Factory

- **Website:** www.funfactory.com
- **Description:** Fun Factory offers high-quality, German-engineered sex toys known for their playful designs and powerful

performance. They emphasize body-safe materials and user-friendly products.

12. Je Joue

- **Website:** www.jejoue.com
- **Description:** Je Joue is a luxury brand offering elegantly designed sex toys that focus on pleasure and ergonomics. Their products are known for their sophisticated look and high performance.

13. Dame Products

- **Website:** www.dameproducts.com
- **Description:** Dame Products is a women-founded company that designs innovative and user-friendly sex toys. They focus on creating products that enhance pleasure and intimacy for all genders.

14. b-Vibe

- **Website:** www.bvibe.com
- **Description:** b-Vibe specializes in high-quality anal toys, including vibrating anal plugs and prostate massagers. Their products are designed with comfort and safety in mind, offering a range of sizes and features.

15. Satisfyer

- **Website:** www.satisfyer.com
- **Description:** Satisfyer is known for its innovative air pulse technology, providing unique clitoral stimulation. They offer a variety of models and features to cater to different preferences.

Brick-and-Mortar Stores

16. Babeland (Seattle, New York City)

- **Description:** Babeland's physical stores provide a welcoming and educational environment where customers can browse products, attend workshops, and receive personalized recommendations from knowledgeable staff.

17. Good Vibrations (San Francisco, Berkeley, Oakland, Palo Alto, Boston)

- **Description:** Good Vibrations' stores offer a wide selection of sex toys, books, and accessories, along with in-store workshops and events to educate and empower customers.

18. The Pleasure Chest (Los Angeles, New York City, Chicago, West Hollywood)

- **Description:** The Pleasure Chest's stores are known for their inclusive and supportive atmosphere, offering a diverse range of products and hosting educational workshops and events.

19. Smitten Kitten (Minneapolis)

- **Description:** Smitten Kitten's physical store provides a curated selection of body-safe sex toys and promotes sexual health and education through workshops and events.

20. She Bop (Portland)

- **Description:** She Bop is a women-owned sex toy boutique offering a carefully curated selection of body-safe products. They provide a welcoming space for all genders and orientations, with a focus on education and empowerment.

Discreet and Inclusive Retailers

21. Unbound

- **Website:** www.unboundbabes.com
- **Description:** Unbound offers a range of sex toys and accessories, emphasizing inclusivity and body positivity. They are known for their discreet packaging and playful, feminist approach to sexuality.

22. Wild Flower

- **Website:** www.wildflowersex.com
- **Description:** Wild Flower is an inclusive sex shop offering a variety of toys, accessories, and educational resources. They focus on celebrating diverse sexualities and providing a safe and supportive shopping experience.

23. Sugar (Baltimore)

- **Website:** www.sugartheshop.com
- **Description:** Sugar is a feminist sex toy shop that offers a wide range of body-safe products and provides sex-positive education through workshops and events.

24. Early to Bed (Chicago)

- **Website:** www.early2bed.com
- **Description:** Early to Bed is a women-owned sex shop that offers a carefully curated selection of toys, books, and accessories. They focus on promoting sexual health and pleasure through education and community involvement.

25. Self Serve Toys (Albuquerque)

- **Website:** www.selfservetoys.com
- **Description:** Self Serve Toys is a sex-positive retailer that offers a range of body-safe products, emphasizing education and empowerment. They provide a welcoming space for all customers to explore their sexual desires.

These retailers provide a diverse selection of high-quality sex toys, accessories, and educational resources. Whether you prefer to shop online or visit a physical store, these recommended retailers ensure you can find the perfect products to enhance your sexual journey. Remember to prioritize body-safe materials, read reviews, and explore educational resources to make informed choices and enjoy a fulfilling and satisfying sexual experience.

Message from the Author:

I hope you enjoyed this book, I love astrology and knew there was not a book such as this out on the shelf. I love metaphysical items as well. Please check out my other books:

-Life of Government Benefits

-My life of Hell

-My life with Hydrocephalus

-Red Sky

-World Domination:Woman's rule

-World Domination:Woman's Rule 2: The War

-Life and Banishment of Apophis: book 1

-The Kidney Friendly Diet

-The Ultimate Hemp Cookbook

-Creating a Dispensary(legally)

-Cleanliness throughout life: the importance of showering from childhood to adulthood.

-Strong Roots: The Risks of Overcoddling children

-Hemp Horoscopes: Cosmic Insights and Earthly Healing

- Celestial Hemp Navigating the Zodiac: Through the Green Cosmos

-Astrological Hemp: Aligning The Stars with Earth's Ancient Herb

-The Astrological Guide to Hemp: Stars, Signs, and Sacred Leaves

-Green Growth: Innovative Marketing Strategies for your Hemp Products and Dispensary

-Cosmic Cannabis

-Astrological Munchies

-Henry The Hemp

-Zodiacal Roots: The Astrological Soul Of Hemp

- **Green Constellations: Intersection of Hemp and Zodiac**

-Hemp in The Houses: An astrological Adventure Through The Cannabis Galaxy

-Galactic Ganja Guide

Heavenly Hemp

Zodiac Leaves

Doctor Who Astrology

Cannastrology

Stellar Satvias and Cosmic Indicas

Celestial Cannabis: A Zodiac Journey

AstroHerbology: The Sky and The Soil: Volume 1

AstroHerbology:Celestial Cannabis:Volume 2

Cosmic Cannabis Cultivation

The Starry Guide to Herbal Harmony: Volume 1

The Starry Guide to Herbal Harmony: Cannabis Universe: Volume 2

Yugioh Astrology: Astrological Guide to Deck, Duels and more

Nightmare Mansion: Echoes of The Abyss

Nightmare Mansion 2: Legacy of Shadows

Nightmare Mansion 3: Shadows of the Forgotten

Nightmare Mansion 4: Echoes of the Damned

The Life and Banishment of Apophis: Book 2

Nightmare Mansion: Halls of Despair

Healing with Herb: Cannabis and Hydrocephalus

Planetary Pot: Aligning with Astrological Herbs: Volume 1

Fast Track to Freedom: 30 Days to Financial Independence Using AI, Assets, and Agile Hustles

Cosmic Hemp Pathways

How to Become Financially Free in 30 Days: 10,000 Paths to Prosperity

Zodiacal Herbage: Astrological Insights: Volume 1

Nightmare Mansion: Whispers in the Walls

The Daleks Invade Atlantis

Henry the hemp and Hydrocephalus

10X The Kidney Friendly Diet

Cannabis Universe: Adult coloring book

Hemp Astrology: The Healing Power of the Stars

Zodiacal Herbage: Astrological Insights: Cannabis Universe: Volume 2

Planetary Pot: Aligning with Astrological Herbs: Cannabis Universes: Volume 2

Doctor Who Meets the Replicators and SG-1: The Ultimate Battle for Survival

Nightmare Mansion: Curse of the Blood Moon

The Celestial Stoner: A Guide to the Zodiac

Check out my Virtual dispensary for all your hemp needs: https://shift.store/sg1fan23477/retail

If you want solar for your home go here: https://www.harborsolar.live/apophisenterprises/

Get Some Tarot cards: https://www.makeplayingcards.com/sell/apophis-occult-shop

Get some shirts: https://www.bonfire.com/store/apophis-shirt-emporium/

Instagrams:
@apophis_enterprises,
@hempkingdom2024,
@apophisbookemporium,
@apophisfashion,
@apophisscardshop

Twitter: @apophisenterpr1,

Tiktok:@apophisenterprise

Youtube: @sg1fan23477
@FiresideRetreatKingdom

Podcast: ApophisChatZone: https://open.spotify.com/show/5zXbrCLEV2xzCp8ybrfHsk?si=fb4d4fdbdce44dec

Newsletter: https://apophiss-newsletter-27c897.beehiiv.com/